A Short History of Hilton Head Island

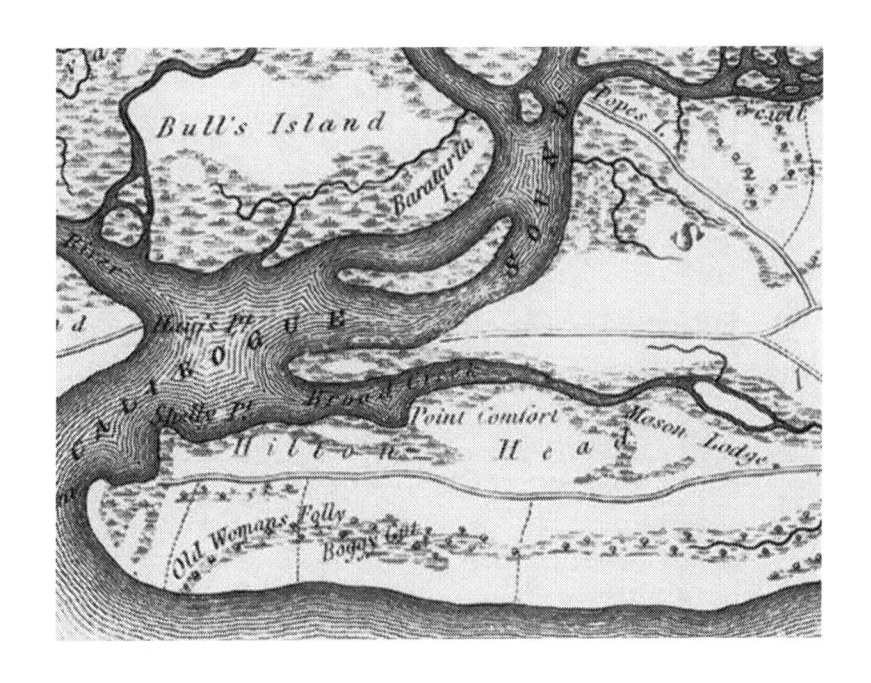

David B. McCoy

Acknowledgements:

Thanks to my proofreaders, Mary Ann D'Aurelio, David Huthmacher, and Dr. Rhonda Baughman for proofreading the revised, 2014, draft; the staffs at the Hilton Head Library and the Heritage Library; the Hilton Head Island-Bluffton Chamber of Commerce; Bobbe Carota; Kathy Powers; Carla Sikorski Kirby; Mary Ann Browning Ford of the Hilton Head Island Land Trust; Natalie Hefter of the Coastal Discovery Museum, Hilton Head Island, SC.,

---

"The Mystery of the GREYTON H. TAYLOR Monument" was written with assistance from Steve Riley, Hilton Head Island Town Manager; Lynn W. Buchman, Hilton Head Administrative Assistant - Executive Department; Paul Sprague, museum director of The Greyton H. Taylor Wine Museum; and Katie Threatt, Charter One Realty.

A Short History of Hilton Head Island, 3rd Ed.
© David B. McCoy, 2012, 2014, 2017, 2018.

ISBN-10: 1521105324
ISBN-13: 978-1521105320

Spare Change Press ™
Massillon, Ohio
scp-iyh-staff@yandex.com
sparechangepress.com

Introduction

Over the span of fifteen years, my wife and I vacationed on Hilton Head Island at least ten times. Like most visitors, once arriving we settled into a comfortable routine: after breakfast we headed for the beach; around noon, we were ready to go in for some wine and cheese—maybe even a short nap; by 6 P.M., we were enjoying dinner at one the island's many fine restaurants. We knew the island had a number of golf courses, miles of bike paths, privately gated "plantations," and tall foliage preventing us from seeing any store we were trying to find on Williams Hilton Parkway. But that all changed a few years ago.

Two years after retiring, I spent three months on the island during the winter months. Being from Ohio, that certainly proved to be a wonderful experience—so much so, I began looking for property we could afford. Due to a depressed housing market, I found a comfortable condo on the marsh side of the island. About the same time, I joined an organization called Road Scholars (formally known as Elder Hostels). They offer a variety of vacations that include lectures given by professors and experts related to the particular adventure.

Looking through their catalog soon after buying our condo, I discovered that Road Scholars offers a week-long workshop/vacation relating to Hilton Head Island. This turned out to be a real eye-opener for me. What had once been just a remarkable vacation site became an island with a long and fascinating history. My interest piqued, I sought out books related to the island's history, but found that none have been written since 1989.

A Short History of Hilton Head Island is my attempt to bring you the rich history of Hilton Head Island in a short, concise and informative way.

Topics covered:

- Shell Rings of Hilton Head Island
- An Age of Exploration
- Europeans Come to the Carolina Region
- The Spanish, the French, the British
- The Indigo Years
- Revolution on the Island
- Sea Island Cotton Years
- The Plantation Task System
- Civil War Battle of Port Royal
- Mitchelville, an Experiment in Citizenship
- Civil War forts Howell and Mitchel
- Years of Isolation
- Gullah Heritage
- Charles E. Fraser and Two Decades of Change
- Paradise Almost Lost
- The Mystery of the Greyton H. Taylor Monument
- Hilton Head Island Time Line

Shell Rings of Hilton Head Island

Nomadic hunters from northeast Asia crossed the Bering Strait land bridge during the Ice Age, and over thousands of years, spread across North and South America. When first arriving in North America, their diets remained heavily based on the large animals they had followed across the strait. But, for reasons unknown, these mammoths, great sloths, saber-tooth cats, camels, and wild horses became extinct. This then led to hunting and gathering of smaller animals and plants. The first of these humans arrived in South Carolina at least 13,000 years ago at the tail end of the glacial period.

As tribes migrated to the Atlantic Coast, by the Late Archaic-Early Woodland period (LA-EW), natives began devising methods to exploit the area's abundant oyster beds. This allowed them to give up the migratory hunting and gathering life-style that preceded them for permanent and semi-permanent settlements. Freed from having to be constantly moving, they became the first to build permanent structures called shell rings, or shell middens, that would set into motion the mound-building tradition of the Middle Woodland and Mississippian periods. These LA-EW inhabitants would also become the first to make and use ceramics and pottery in North America.

Twenty shell rings from the LA-EW period, 3000 BCE to 1 CE, have been identified in South Carolina, and two are located on Hilton Head Island. The term "ring" is a bit misleading because not all middens (referring to waste from food sources) are circular. Some are oval, elliptical or donut-shaped; others are crescent-shaped. The outer rim-to-rim diameters of rings are generally 50 to 300 feet. They have been found to be from two to ten feet in height and between 10 to 30 feet in width.

Postholes from occupied structures have been found within a few rings. Pits used for roasting and steaming of food were a common feature of ring sites. Some pits were used for underground storage only and not for cooking. The interior of most rings was kept relatively free of shells and used as a public space. The precise nature of the gatherings remains unknown, but dancing, marriage, and public oratory seem likely. South Carolina rings are primarily composed of the American oyster, hard-shelled and razor clams, whelks, ribbed mussels, fish bones, as well as bones from deer, birds, raccoons, rabbits, opossum and other animal remains.

In addition to food refuse, significantly fashioned artifacts have been found. Shells were crafted into a large number of tools used in constructing rings, providing of food, and in the cooking and serving of food. Shells of bivalves (scallops, clams, oysters, mussels) were perforated and used as weights for fishing nets. They were also notched and sharpened to make hoes, adzes and celts (an early type of ax); however, these tools were not used in the planting and harvesting of crops. Whelks and conch shells were ground down and fashioned into fish hooks, chisels, and hammers to cull oysters. Sometimes the whorls of whelks and conchs were squared off and worked into spoons, dippers, and scoops.

Other fashioned artifacts that have been discovered are fiber-tempered ceramic shards which were first formally identified in 1943 at the Chester Field shell ring on Port Royal Island, near Beaufort, South Carolina. Known as Stallings Plain ceramics, they were made by mixing clay with fibers from Spanish moss or Saw Palmetto and firing it. The fibers functioned as a temper and kept the pot from cracking during the firing process. Firing made the pot hard and waterproof. Early pottery from this period tended to be plain, but in time decorative lines and patterns were scratched or pressed into the wet clay.

The purpose of shell rings is unknown, although rings appear to be carefully planned and systematically deposited structures. The builders initially stacked shells in small piles seven to eight feet in diameter in the shape of a ring. Next, they added shells to fill in the gaps until the entire ring was complete. And finally, they smoothed the top with a layer of crushed shells and soil. While it is always romantic to tie some higher significance to things, there appears to be none with shell rings. They simply appear to mark a central gathering or living point for the tribe and were simply the inhabitants' creative means of discarding refuse.

Two shell midden formations from the LA-EW period are found on Hilton Head Island. The Skull Creek structure is located on Squire Pope Road, but it is closed to the public. This is an interesting site because it appears to be donut-shaped, but it is in fact one ring superimposed over an earlier ring. The southernmost ring has suffered extensive removal of shells probably due to the shells being used in the form of tabby for roads and building. (Tabby is a building material consisting of lime, sand, water, and crushed oyster shells.) The smaller northern ring is nearly plowed level with the surrounding farm land.

The second midden formation is the shell ring in the Sea Pines Forest Preserve. The ring itself has an average diameter of 136 feet and a height of two feet. As other rings, it is composed primarily of oyster shells, as well as pottery shards and animal bones. This ring is open to the public dawn to dusk.[i]

A third midden formation, from the Mississippian period, is also located on Squire Pope Road, just west of Rt. 278. Known as Green's Shell Enclosure, it too is open to the public. Green's Shell Enclosure is a semi-circular ridge of shells 20 to 30 feet wide at the base and four feet high. By the time it was built and inhabited (1300-1500 CE), the tribes had become less nomadic, more agricultural, and highly protective of their land. The outer semi-circular ridge would have been topped by a wooden palisade. In the center, part of the outer crest juts in, and a few feet away rests an oval-shaped mound which probably served as a raised platform for the chief's house. To get to the site, one walks through a fence and past a Gullah cemetery.

Native Americans would continue to be the main inhabitants of Hilton Head and the surrounding Sea Islands until the Yemasee Wars in the early 1700s.

Related YouTube videos:
"Archaeology students excavate the Sea Pines Indian shell ring"
"Shell Ring - The Sea Pines Resort - Hilton Head Island"

An Age of Exploration

In 1095 CE, Pope Urban II declared a Crusade, or holy war, to win back the Holy Land from the Muslims. For a period of 200 years, there were nine crusades. While the Crusades may have failed to accomplish their religious objective, they had considerable impact on the European culture.

The Muslims, for years, had imported the riches from India, China, and eastern Africa for their own pleasure. While fighting in the Holy Land, Crusaders learned from their Muslim enemy about something European people dearly craved—spices. With a diet made up largely of bread, gruel, and meat (either heavily salted or rancid from lack of refrigeration) such things as pepper, cloves, sugar, nutmeg, and other spices must have seemed like, despite the overall failure, a godsend.

And if this was not enough, the latest read was a book by a young man named Marco Polo. In the 1200s, Marco spent 20 years traveling throughout the Far East with his father, a merchant and trader. Once back in Italy, he wrote tales of rich silks, rare spices, gold, jewels and luxurious palaces in his *Descriptions of the World*.

Not wanting to be left behind in the lucrative business of selling these high demand, high priced items, Spain, France, and England decided it was worth the risk to break up the profitable monopolies held by the Ottoman Turks, Italians, and Portuguese. By the 1500s, Turks controlled both the land and waterways east beyond the Mediterranean to Asia. (The Turks would hire Genoese and Venetian vessels to transport the goods throughout the Mediterranean and Black Seas region. In exchange for distributing goods, the Italians took payment in the form of gold and a share of the cargo to sell for profit.) The Portuguese had, under the guidance of Henry the Navigator, sailed around the tip of Africa by way of portolan sailing (in other words, never losing sight of land). This left only one way to get to the East: go east by sailing west.

That simple phrase, go east by sailing west, raised two serious questions, though. Just how big was the Atlantic Ocean, and could a ship carry enough food and water to reach Asia? Also, once they reached Asia, could they sail back to Europe? Christopher Columbus was the only person who thought he knew the answers to these questions. Columbus had sailed all the way to Ireland, and maybe Iceland, and heard stories of lands west, so he reasoned that Asia couldn't be that far off. He also had picked up from experience, and from Portuguese sailors he met, the patterns of the prevailing/trade winds that blow in the Atlantic. Those in the low latitude blow west, and those in the mid-latitude region blow east. With these bits of knowledge, and his many years of being a sailor, he was able to convince Ferdinand and Isabella of Spain to support his voyage.

In time, Spain, France, and Great Britain would all sail across the Atlantic to build colonies which gave them great wealth. Spain would conquer the Native Americas in Central and South America for their gold and silver; France would settle Canada and grow wealthy from beaver pelts (used to make the new stylish tri-corn hat) and fish; Great Britain would settle along the Atlantic Coast of North America for its abundant natural resources. In their struggle to expand their empires and wealth, all would sail off the shores of Hilton Head Island.

Europeans Come to the Carolina Region

The first effort to colonize Carolina was made by a Spanish lawyer and government official in Santo Domingo named Lucas Vasquez de Ayllón. In 1521, de Ayllón funded an expedition that headed north along the coast looking for land suitable for settlement. Because official government business prevented him from going along, he hired Francisco Gordillo to serve as captain. (Cordillo Parkway is named in honor of Gordillo, but somewhere along the way the "G" was changed to "C".) Before leaving the Bahamas, Gordillo was joined by another ship under the command of Pedro de Quexos. As reported back to de Ayllón, the two ships spent months exploring the Atlantic Coast, but when a storm blew up, Gordillo and his ship were lost. De Quexos continued with the project and when the winds settled down, he saw before him a bold bluff headland topped with tall green trees. Sailing closer, he saw the entrance to a wide harbor, and marveled at never having seen any harbor or any land look so fair. It is speculated that the wide harbor he encountered was Port Royal Sound, and the bold bluff was the northeast corner of Hilton Head Island. Moving on, de Quexos briefly stepped ashore on either present-day South Carolina or George, and claimed the land for Spain, the Holy Catholic Church, and de Ayllón. On that day, August 18, 1521, and after ascertaining his latitude as 32 degrees north, he and his men set sail for Santo Domingo.

With such encouraging accounts, de Ayllón applied for a royal commission to explore the Carolina coast further and to establish a settlement he would name San Miguel de Gualdape. In July 1526, de Ayllón sailed from the port of La Plata in Hispaniola with six good-sized ships and six hundred men and women. He also brought a number of slaves and one hundred good horses (which are believed to be the Marsh Tacky horses still found on Hilton Head Island today). Not finding the first site of landfall to his liking, de Ayllón settled on or near Georgia's Sapelo Island. Once settled, the colony of 600 people encountered hunger, disease, scarcity of supplies, death and troubles with the local natives. After three months, and the death of de Ayllón from malaria, the 150 survivors made their way back to Hispaniola that winter.

A few other attempts were made by the Spanish to settle along the Carolina coast, but all failed. Then, for more than 40 years, Spanish ships explored no further than La Florida until a group of French Protestants, called Huguenots, showed interest in settling the Carolina area. (Spanish vessels did continue to sail off Carolina until they were far enough north to pick up the trade winds back to Spain.) For the Indians in the area, life returned to normal. They lived in peace and continued their ceremony of drinking a black tea of holly leaves and stems which induced hallucinations and vomiting. In their own language, the Indians called the brew 'white drink' because white symbolizes purity, happiness, social harmony, but the Spanish called it 'black drink' because of its color. Europeans incorrectly believed that vomiting was caused by the plant, hence the Latin name of the plant, Ilex vomitoria. However, the active ingredient was actually caffeine, and the vomiting was either learned behavior or a result of the great quantities in which they drank coupled with fasting.

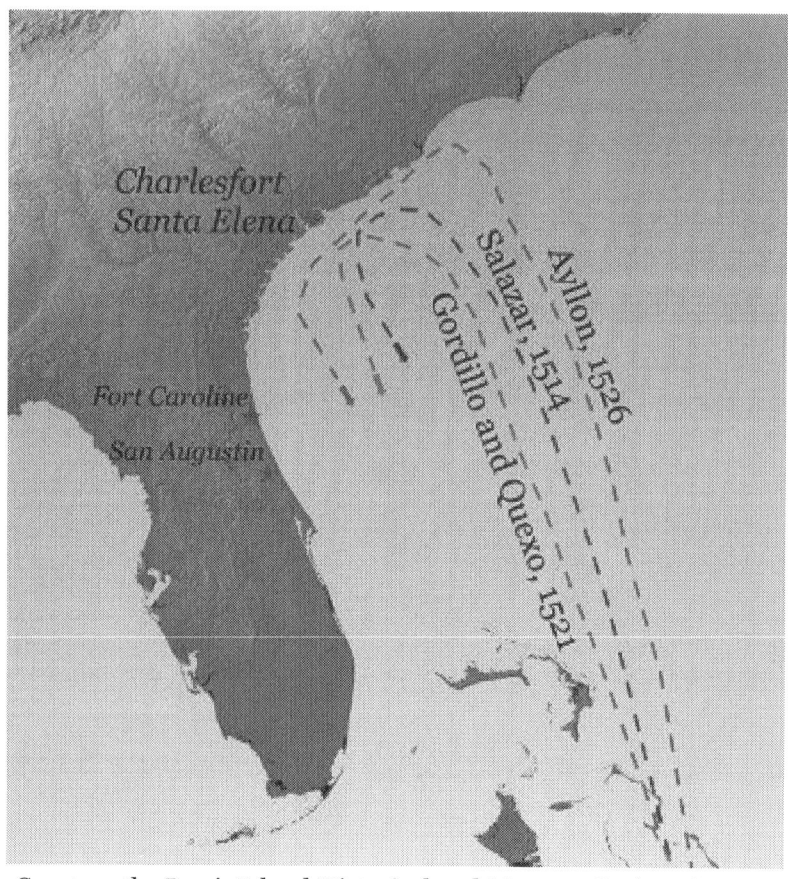

Courtesy the Parris Island Historical and Museum Society © 2009

The French

Competition in trade, especially with Portugal, led French merchants and financiers from Lyon and Rouen to encourage King Francis I of France to fund an expedition to discover new trade routes to Asia. After several false starts, Giovanni da Verrazzano, an Italian explorer, departed under the French flag on January 17, 1524. His orders were to explore and claim North America, with the main goal of finding a sea route to the Pacific Ocean and ultimately China. In March, Verrazzano neared the area of Cape Fear, and after a short stay, reached modern North Carolina and the Pamlico Sound lagoon before continuing to explore the coast further northward to Newfoundland. When he returned to France in July 1524, Verrazzano named the region he explored Francesca in honor of the French king; however, Verrazzano's brother's map labeled it 'Nova Gallia', New France.

Shortly before this, in October 1517, Martin Luther of Germany set into motion the Protestant Reformation. Fueled by the protests against the abuses and teachings of the Catholic Church, Protestantism rapidly spread to France, which was strictly ruled by Catholic Monarchs. The reign of Francis I (1515-47) began the persecution of Protestants, known as Huguenots, and under Henry II (1547-59), attacks intensified with the formation of government policy allowing for the trial and execution of heretics.

As luck would have it, Protestant Huguenots found support in Gaspard de Coligny. His mother came from the old and powerful French Montmorency family. During Coligny's youth, his uncle was one of the most influential figures in the courts of Francis I and Henry II. Because of his kinship with the Montmorencys, de Gaspard was named Admiral of France and governor of two major French provinces. As admiral, he became France's first active proponent of colonial expansion in the New World. Between 1555 and 1571, he authorized and supported several colonizing expeditions. His intent was to establish a French foothold whereby they could prey on the Spanish fleets returning to Spain, establish a permanent settlement in North America, and help Huguenots establish their own colonies to escape persecution. Sometime around 1546, de Coligny had converted to Calvinism but did not officially announce his support for the Reformation until 1560.

In February 1562, two ships under the command of Jean Ribaut, and one hundred and fifty men, left Havre de Grace in Normandy, Frace bound for Florida. On May 1, they entered the St. Johns River near modern-day Jacksonville. Even though La Florida had been claimed by Spain, Ribaut ordered the erection of a heavy stone marker denoting France's claim. After a brief stopover, he headed north.

On May 17, the two French ships entered the wide harbor de Quexos may have discovered, and "because of the largenesse and fairness thereof," named it "Port Royale." Perhaps Ribaut was indeed impressed by what he saw, but the harbor's existence was known to him by way of a map he had somehow acquired before leaving France.

Not wanting to be discovered by Spanish ships, Ribaut sailed some nine miles up the channel. There he found the natives to be friendly and happy to supply them with needed food, and thus concluded this was an ideal spot for a French settlement. After appointing Albert de la Pierria to command the colony, Ribaut left twenty-six volunteers behind to complete the construction of a wooden outpost on what is now Parris

Island. They named their little settlement Charlesfort in honor of the French King Charles IX (1561-1574). Expecting a speedy return of Ribaut with resupplies of food and more settlers, the men of Charlesfort saw no need to plant crops, or to salt and stockpile game or fish.

Upon reaching Europe, Ribaut found himself embroiled in political and religious turmoil and was prevented from returning to Charlesfort. Six months passed and both the settlers and the nearby Indians were running out of food, so they visited other tribes to beg for food. As was the custom among Native Americans, food was readily shared, but this would only create false hopes. Convinced now they had enough stores to see them through to Ribaut's return, they again made no effort to plant crops.

When hunger returned, quarrels and insubordination arose. Their commander, la Pierria, responded harshly—hanging one man and exiling another named Lachere. Finally, the men revolted, killed la Pierria, and elected Nicholas Barre as their new commander. After sizing up the situation and seeing it as hopeless, Barre decided they had to return to France.

Constructing a ship described to be a 20-ton vessel with one mast (200-ton was an average-sized ship at the time), a set of oars, and a sail made from their own bedding and shirts, the remaining 21 men set out in the spring of 1563. The voyage turned out to be a difficult one, and when their food was depleted, they turned to eating their shoes and other leather goods. But that too was not enough to keep them alive. In ultimate desperation, the decision was made to sacrifice one of their own. Lachere, who had been banished by la Pierria and rescued, drew the short lot, making it possible for the remaining seven to survive until they were rescued by an English ship.

After this mishap, the French would again sail to the southern coast of North America, but they were never to return to Port Royale. And their sponsor, Gaspard de Coligny, would fair no better. He became the main target of the St. Bartholomew's Day Massacre when Catholics killed a large number of Huguenots gathered in August 1572 for the wedding of the Queen's sister to the future Protestant King Henry IV.

The Spanish Return

The presence of French Huguenots along the Atlantic coast caused two serious problems for Spain. First, the Protestant faith was broadening its reach to the New World. Second, Spanish ships, heading north to the mid-latitude to take advantage of the west-blowing winds, would be in constant danger of being attacked.

Hoping to resolve both issues, in the spring of 1566, Pedro Menendez de Aviles sailed north and built a fort the new settlers called San Felipe. (In fact, they built their fort overtop Charlesfort obviating any claim the French might wish to make.) They also gave Hilton Head Island the name Isla de Los Osos—Island of Bears. It is believed that while the island was never settled by the Spanish, they utilized its resources. The island at the time was plentiful with animals, and Spanish Wells served as a source of fresh water.

By July, a group of some 250 men, women, and children arrived. When news that San Felipe and the surrounding lands were "good for bread and wind and all kinds of livestock" reached Spain, more people joined the colony. But unlike the friendly relationships the French enjoyed with the Indians, the Spanish demanded too much and mistreated the tribes. Tensions finally reached the boiling point in 1576 when Fort San Felipe was surrounded and burned.

Refusing to abandon the idea of building a colony in Carolina, the King ordered a new fort constructed. Not far from the remains of San Felipe, 60 houses were built from tabby cement and the colony was renamed San Marcos. This settlement would survive ten years before it, too, would fall at the hands of the surrounding tribes.

The British Arrive

By 1662, British colonies had been established in New England, New York, Delaware, Maryland, and Virginia. Also, by this time, the monarchy had been restored after the English Civil War, and Charles II was king. Three years after the restoration, eight men who had helped Charles II regain his crown demanded payment in the form of land they believed would insure them and their heirs permanent wealth. Because it cost the King nothing to give away unoccupied land in America, he issued a charter on March 24, 1663 creating the eight as Lord Proprietors of Carolina.

To the dismay of the Proprietors, there was little interest in England to settle in Carolina, but that was not the case in Barbados. Sugar and rice planters there were finding land increasingly scarce and were eager to find more extensive and cheaper land. Out of frustration, a few moved to Jamaica, but others set their sights on the greater opportunities that the mainland of North America promised. Some of these Barbadians hoped that if they funded a voyage of discovery, the Lord Proprietors would grant them free land for their efforts.

The young sea captain they hired was one of the most skilled mariners in the American Colonies and had already explored the area of Cape Fear, North Carolina in 1662. The expedition, under the command of Captain William Hilton, left Barbados on August 10, 1663. On September 3, he sailed into St. Helena Sound which is some 30 miles north of Hilton Head Island. Upon arriving, he began to explore the area and was greeted by the area's Native Americans. They informed Hilton that several English sailors that had recently ship-wrecked were living with them. Because the Indians failed to produce any sailors, Hilton spent nearly a month exploring the area in long-boats. For all his efforts, he was able to find and rescue only two of the supposedly thirteen castaways.

Satisfied with the information he accumulated about St. Helena and Parris Islands, and the Port Royal Sound from inland waterways, he decided to investigate the Sound's seaward approach. Sailing south from St. Helena Sound, Hilton came upon an unnamed island and noticed a high bluff at the southern entrance of the large Port Royal Sound. In his sea log, he noted that by keeping the bluff headland, "Hilton Head," as a landmark, a mariner could find safe entry into the Sound.

For four days Hilton investigated the island with the high bluff, recording all he saw. His observations, though, were cut short when a violent storm sent his ships seeking safety out at sea. Hilton's report was well received by his Barbados sponsors and the Lord Proprietors. A year later, it was published in London to advertise the infinite opportunities of Carolina. In part it read:

The Lands are laden with large tall Oaks, Walnut and Bayes, except facing on the Sea, it is most Pines tall and good...The Land generally, is a good Soyl...The Indians plant in the worst Land, because they cannot cut down the Timber in the best, and yet have plenty of Corn, Pumpions, Water-Mellons, Musk-Mellons. The Country abounds with Grapes, large Figs, and Peaches; the Woods with Deer, Conies, Turkeys, Quails Curlues, Plovers, Teile, Herons; and as the Indians say, in Winter, with Swans, Geese, Cranes, Duck and Mallard, and innumerable of other water-Fowls. The Rivers stored plentifully with Fish that we saw play and leap. The Ayr is clear and sweet, the Countrey very pleasant and delightful: And we could wish, that all they that want a happy settlement, of our English Nation, were well transported thither.

Despite the interest raised in England and Barbados, it was not until March 1670 that 100 settlers reached Port Royal Sound. These were to be the vanguard of South Carolina's colonial population, but they decided Hilton Head Island was an undesirable place to settle. In their meetings with the region's Native Americans, they learned the area was unsafe due to Spaniards, man-eating Westo Indians, and frequent hurricanes. (In fact, Hilton Head Island was still under Spanish control and not granted to the British under the recently signed Anglo-Spanish Treaty of Madrid.)

Taking their given advice seriously, the group made their way to the Ashley River and settled at a place they called Albemarle Point. The Proprietors, however, renamed it Charles Town in honor of the King. (Ironically, William Hilton would also be one to reject the island for Charles Town.) Thus, Hilton Head Island would remain in Indian and Spanish hands for another fifty years, but during that span of years, two events transpired that would make settlement possible. First, on August 16, 1698, the Proprietors awarded John Bayley of Ireland a barony, or grant of 48,000 acres which included land on the area's sea island and mainland. And second, by 1717, wars between the Yamasee and Tuscarora Indians, and the conflict between the Yamasee and European settlers came to an end. In part, peace came due to the campaigns led by Colonel John Barnwell. Barnwell led campaigns in late 1711 and early 1712, with an army mostly made up of Yamasee Indians against the Tuscarora Indians who were attacking both the English and the Yamasee. For winning battles against insurmountable odds, Barnwell earned the nickname "Tuscarora Jack," and was awarded 1,000 acres on the northwest tip of Hilton Head Island. Today, "Tuscarora Jack" Barnwell is acknowledged as Hilton Head Island's first white settler.

War between the Yamasee and European settlers resulted due to the influx of white settlers taking Yamasee farming and hunting lands. Adding to this, Natives began buying goods from the British and paying them with deerskins. Over-hunting, though, caused the Yamasee to fall behind in payments, so the British began enslaving Yamasee women and children to cover outstanding debts. In the spring of 1715, the Yamasee formed a confederation with other tribes and struck at the white settlements in South Carolina. Several hundred settlers were killed, homes were burned, and livestock slaughtered. At first, it appeared the Yamasee were going to overwhelm the settlers, but when colonists from North Carolina and Virginia joined the fight, they were slowly pushed south through Georgia back into their ancestral lands in northern Florida. There, the tribe was virtually annihilated by the Creek Indians.

While John Bayley was granted most of Hilton Head Island, he took no interest in it, and the land passed to his son, John. Son John also had no use for the land and hired Alexander Trench, formerly from Dublin, Ireland, as his real estate agent. Inept as a salesman, Trench used Hilton Head for grazing his own cattle and the island became known locally as "Trench's Island." While Trench never made any claim to the land, his name remained on some maps up to the early 1800s.

While Trench failed to sell land for the Barleys, he did rent much of the land out for them. By 1766, twenty-five families were operating plantations on the island. These settlers took to growing the indigo plant to make a highly-prized blue dye and embraced the Patriots' cause for independence. Both choices would be put to the test when war came.

The Indigo Years

Unlike the coastal regions along the Carolinas that grew rice, Hilton Head Island's lack of readily accessible fresh water made indigo the cash crop of choice during the 1700s. The success of indigo became a major source of wealth largely due to Eliza Lucas.

When Eliza's mother's health deteriorated while living on the island of Antigua, her father, Lt. Colonel George Lucas, relocated the family to South Carolina in 1738. Upon arriving, George purchased three plantations, but soon discovered that rice could not be cultivated on one of them. Before having any chance of settling in, George was called back to Antigua to serve as governor—leaving 16-year-old Eliza to manage the household and plantations.

This was not a hasty decision on George's part. Eliza was a well-read young woman, educated in England, and an amateur botanist. Despite being unable to grow rice on the one plantation, she was determined to find a suitable crop that would. After three years of experiments with the French tropical indigo, she finally developed a variety that could stand the periodic frost of the temperate South Carolina climate. More remarkable, she decided against keeping the discovery to herself.

Eliza used most of her 1744 crop to make seed which she shared with planters facing the same hurdles she faced growing rice. Her development caught the attention of Parliament, who grew tired of buying indigo from the French, and authorized a six-penny per pound subsidy to American growers. This set into motion the 30-year "Indigo Bonanza" when planters could double their investment every three to four years. However, turning the indigo plant into a useable dye was an intensive slave-labor process. What follows is a short description of the process as described by Jean M. West:

Slaves placed the cut indigo in the "steeper," a large tub filled with water and sank the plants with logs or stones. In about 12-24 hours, the indigo began to ferment, making the water bubble and turn amber-green as it drew the pigment grain from the leaves. Although the colonial dye-makers described the putrid smell of the rotting indigo, they did not realize that the indigo was oxidizing, forming a liquid chemical now known as indican.

The fermented mixture was drawn down into the second "beater" vat where trash was picked out of the liquid and it was churned with paddles by the slaves to add oxygen until it turned green and then violet-blue, around two hours. Continued churning caused the indigo to condense into specks, then flakes, which sank like mud to the bottom of the vat, separating from the now clear water.

The water was drawn into the third container, leaving the indigo at the bottom of the second vat. Slaves spooned the pudding-consistency indigo into cloth bags to drain overnight. The next day, they packed the blue mud into square, brick-size containers with drainage holes. After additional pressing and drying, slaves removed the indigo from the molds and cut it into squares roughly 1½ inches in size. When completely dry, premium pieces of "pigeon neck" indigo were a sparkling, iridescent dark blue, light in weight and very hard.

Indigo dye is not water soluble (the reason why it separates in the second vat) so when ready to be used for dying, it was dissolved in stale urine, tannic acid, or wood-ash. The stinking mixture would then be introduced into water, producing a yellow-green solution. Cloth dipped into the dye solution turned yellow-green until it was removed from the liquid and exposed to oxygen--then, almost magically, as the cloth would dry, it would turn blue.

Related YouTube video:
"Eliza Lucas Pinckney"

Revolution on the Island

The Bonanza period came to an end with the Revolutionary War when Parliament cancelled the indigo subsidy. As for Eliza, she would marry Charles Pinckney in 1744, to whom she bore two sons. Thomas Pinckney fought in the American Revolution and was elected governor of South Carolina 1787-1789. Charles Cotesworth Pinckney also served in the Continental Army and between 1789-1795 served as Secretary of War and Secretary of State. He was twice the Federalist Party nominee for president of the United States. In 1804, he retired to the island that would become commonly known as Pinckney Island, just west of Hilton Head Island, and developed a thriving, long-staple cotton plantation on 297 acres.

The plantation flourished until the Civil War when it was occupied by Union Troops. After the war, the island was virtually abandoned, except for several owners who used it as a hunting preserve. In 1975, the island was donated to the U.S. Fish and Wildlife Service to be managed exclusively as a National Wildlife Refuge and as a nature and forest preserve for aesthetic and conservation purposes. In 1989, Eliza Lucas Pinckney was inducted in to the South Carolina Business Hall of Fame, the first woman so honored.

In addition to destroying the main source of wealth on the island, the inhabitants of Hilton Head also saw their share of Revolutionary War violence. The war had gone badly for the British, so they reasoned that they would have better luck in the South. Once Savannah fell on December 30, 1778, General Augustine Prevost began to plan the invasion of South Carolina. The opening foray of the British invasion took place on Port Royal Island. To get there, on January 29, 1779, the British man-of-war, *HMS Vigilant* was towed through Skull Creek behind Hilton Head Island. The *Vigilant* was a large ship deemed unseaworthy and was put to use as a floating battery. Without sails, it was towed by men in long-boats and was accompanied by several Loyalist privateer crafts. It was these Loyalist privateers who burned all the plantations along Skull Creek and captured over two hundred slaves.

As war consumed South Carolina, Hilton Head Island became a Patriot stronghold, with neighboring Daufuskie Island becoming a British stronghold. To find protection from Patriot raids on the mainland (many of which were carried out by the group known as the Bloody Legion and headquartered on Hilton Head Island), Loyalists tended to gather on Daufuskie Island.

In retaliation for these raids, in November 1781, British Major Maxwell and Loyalist Captain Philip Martinangele of Daufuskie Island led a raiding party to Hilton Head where they burned several homes. Part of their raid included an ambush of Patriots at Two Oaks Plantation near the head of Broad Creek. When two members of the Bloody Legion, riding ahead of the main body, neared the two ancient oaks, a shot rang out hitting the son of a prominent Patriot family of the island, Charles Davant. Before succumbing to death, Charles made it home to tell his son that the man who shot him was Martinagele. In late December, members of the Bloody Legion met to take revenge. Crossing the Calibogue Sound to Daufuskie Island, they surprised Martinagele at his home. Once there, two men grabbed his wife while a third man shot and killed him. They would then go on to plunder the Martinagele plantation of all the family had. Today, a historical marker marking the site of the Two Oaks Ambush can be found at the intersection of Highway 278 and Folly Field Road.

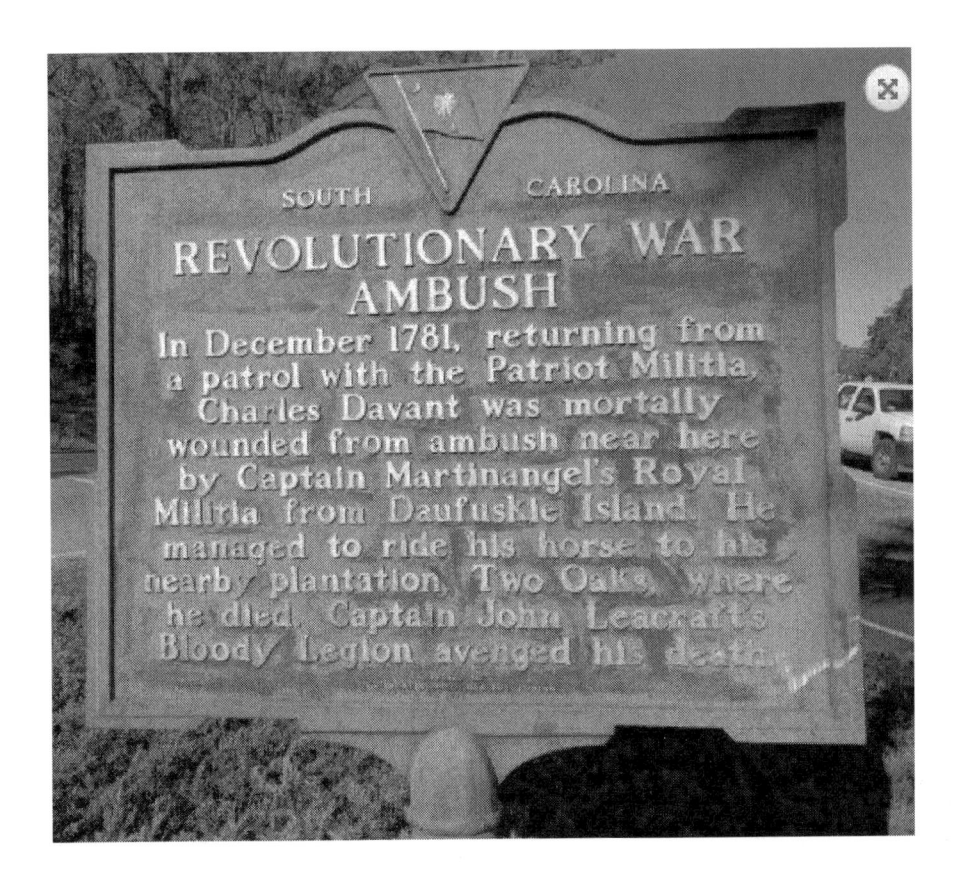

> **SOUTH CAROLINA**
> **REVOLUTIONARY WAR AMBUSH**
> In December 1781, returning from a patrol with the Patriot Militia, Charles Davant was mortally wounded from ambush near here by Captain Martinangel's Royal Militia from Daufuskie Island. He managed to ride his horse to his nearby plantation, Two Oaks, where he died. Captain John Leacraft's Bloody Legion avenged his death.

Sea Island Cotton Years

During the Revolutionary War, most of the major plantations of Hilton Head Island were destroyed. Yet the financial hardship inflicted by the British was short-lived. Around 1785, Georgians imported Sea Island, or long-staple, cotton from the West Indies, and after some difficulty, ushered in the island's most success period of plantation agriculture.

The long-staple plant bears pods of creamy cotton, whose fiber is long, silky and strong. More important, the cotton lint comes away from the seed with relative ease. However, long-staple cotton can only grow along the coasts of Carolina and Georgia because it requires a long-temperate growing season. (The variety of cotton mostly associated with the South is green, or short-staple, cotton. With this variety, the cotton lint sticks tenaciously to the seed, and separating the seed from the lint by hand is tedious and difficult. It would take until 1793, and Eli Whitney's cotton gin, before this cash crop would explode across the landscape and throw the South further into slavery.)

As previously noted, the success of Sea Island cotton came after some experimentation. By 1790, Williams Elliott II of Myrtle Plantation (near Dolphin Head in Hilton Head Plantation) grew the first successful crop on the island. Elliott discovered the key to growing uniformly fine cotton year after year was in selecting the very best seeds for the next crop. The next innovation was introduced by Elliott's neighbor, William Seabrook. Seabrook advocated using salt-marsh muck as fertilizer one year, followed by an application of ground oyster shells the next. A planter using both Elliott's and Seabrook's innovations could dramatically increase his yields and maintain a high-quality product.

With the success of Sea Island cotton, demand for Hilton Head land soared with small planters being bought out and the Bayley barony at last being sold. Principal landholders included Baynard, Chaplin, Drayton, Elliott, Fickling, Gardener, Graham, Jenkins, Kirk, Lawton, Mathew, Pope, Seabrook, Scott, Stoney and Stuart. For the next sixty years, they would reign supreme until the coming of the Civil War and the confiscation of their property by Union forces.

Despite Sea Island cotton turning plantation owners into some of the richest families in the nation, few lived on the island year-round. This, in part, explains why a visitor will not find the remains of any antebellum "Big House" mansions on the island. The wealthiest planters usually had town houses in Beaufort, Charleston, or Savannah. In fact, most rarely visited their plantations at all due to the oppressive heat and fear of diseases.

Less wealthy planters established several summer resort villages within the Beaufort District. At these summer resort villages, planters mingled and socialized with fellow owners, established churches, and exchanged information about business and politics. These resort villages served as the center of white planter society and included St. Helenaville, Blufton, Grahamville and Robertsville to name a few. Generally, these planters would remain in the villages from April until November. They then would pack up and spend Thanksgiving through March at their modest Hilton Head homes.

The island's plantation homes were built on "tabby" foundations, consisting of oyster shells crushed and burned to make lime, then mixed with sand and water. Tabby foundations and walls were often 10-12 inches thick. Several tabby foundations and chimneys can still be found on Squire Pope Road heading north from Rt. 278 right before the traffic rotary, on Baygall Road at Baker Field Park, and on the Stoney-Baynard Ruins in Sea Pines Plantation.[ii] Located off of Plantation Drive in Sea Pines, Baynard Ruins Park is on the right just after passing Baynard Cove Road and Marsh Drive.

The Stoney-Baynard Plantation is an early nineteenth century Sea Island cotton plantation situated on the southwestern end of Hilton Head Island. Most structures were constructed at least partially of tabby, a building material unique to the coastal regions of Florida, Georgia, and southern South Although the history of the Stoney-Baynard Plantation is not perfectly understood, there is good evidence that the plantation was begun in the first quarter of the nineteenth century, perhaps as a speculative venture by its first owners to supply cotton to their factorage. The plantation continued as a large and apparently prosperous holding until Hilton Head fell to Union troops in November 1861.

The oldest intact antebellum structure on the island, also made from tabby, is the Barnard Mausoleum within the Zion Chapel of Ease Cemetery near the intersection of Rt. 278 and Folly Field Road.

Photo by Mike Stroud [VI]

Related YouTube videos:
"Making Tabby Slaking Demonstration"
"Investigating The Tabby Cabins - Kingsley Plantation, Florida" (About the first 3 minutes.)

The Plantation Task System

Sea island cotton planters used the task system of labor management. A "task" was approximately a quarter acre of cultivated land to be worked. Each morning the manager, or driver, would assign a specific task, or tasks, to be completed that day. During the summer months, hoeing weeds was relatively easy, so several tasks might be assigned to slaves. Picking of cotton in the fall was more laborious, so fewer tasks would be assigned. Not only was fieldwork divided by tasks, other plantation jobs were included under the system. Typical production quotas were as follows:

Cutting wood--one cord
Ginning cotton--20-30 pounds per day
Sorting cotton--150-200 pounds per day
Moting (cleaning) cotton--40 pounds per day
Gathering marsh mud for fertilizer--3 cart loads per day

Generally speaking, punishment under the task system was doled out only if slaves failed to complete their assigned daily tasks. In 1850, there were 881 plantations in the Beaufort District with the average number of thirty-four slaves per plantation. There were seventy-nine plantations with more than one hundred slaves, and on Hilton Head Island, this included the Pope, Baynard and Drayton plantations.

The task system encouraged slaves to work hard without supervision. Once hard-working slaves completed their assigned work, they would have the rest of the day to tend their "private field." Many slaves cultivated crops, raised livestock and poultry, and acquired considerable wealth within the slave community. Besides supplementing the daily food ration of corn, slaves could sell their surplus and buy cloth to make clothes or buy domestic items. Many slaves saved enough money to buy more land to add to their private field, which could even be handed down to their children.

An average slave family's private field was four to five acres, but it must not be assumed that slaves actually owned the land. Slaves, and whatever land they "bought," remained the plantation owner's property. This arrangement was embraced by planters because slavery, combined with the task system, provided enormous wealth for planters who were among the richest men in the United States. One owner, Oliver Bostick, pointed out, "it encourages them to do well and be satisfied at home." Yet, what little advantages were gained under the task system, slaves still "endured insult, hardship and abuse under the slave system" (Rowland, Moore and Rogers, 1996).

Battle of Port Royal

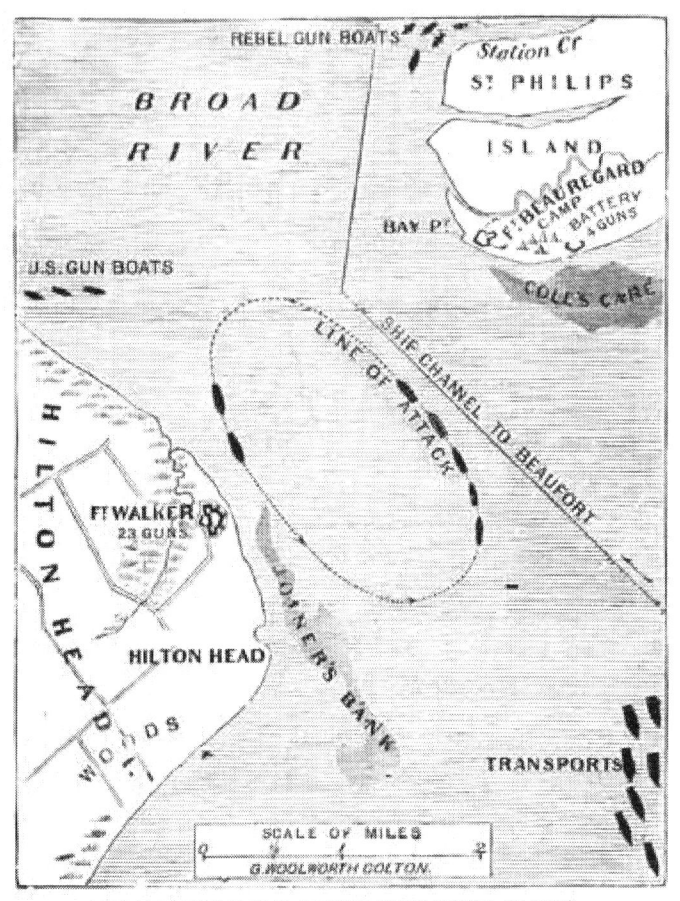

PLAN OF THE NAVAL BATTLE, PORT ROYAL HARBOR.

From November 22, 1861 until January 1872, the island of Hilton Head was renamed Port Royal by General Thomas W. Sherman (not to be confused with William Tecumseh Sherman). Then, as now, when referring to the battle, many thought they were two different places, especially since Port Royal was already the name of the island on which the town of Beaufort was located.

Three days after the fall of Fort Sumter in Charleston Harbor, South Carolina, President Lincoln ordered a blockade of all southern ports. The South's economy was agrarian-based with virtually no factories. Therefore, manufactured goods were purchased from Great Britain with money earned through the sale of cotton. A blockade of Southern ports would greatly cripple the South's war effort.

At first, what became the South Atlantic Blockading Squadron, operated out of the ports of Hampton Roads, Virginia and Key West, Florida. To effectively stop blockade runners, the flotilla would have to interdict illegal shipping without regard to the arbitrary nature of winds and tides. However, this could only be achieved by relying on steam-powered ships and readily available coaling stations and maintenance facilities.

The primary Confederate ports to be blocked were Charleston, South Carolina and Savannah, Georgia. But blockading ships spent as much time traveling to and from their refueling stations as they did on duty. To locate a suitable port to transform into a re-coaling station along the southern coast, the Blockade Strategy Board was created. After much debate, Port Royal Sound and Hilton Head Island were selected. To prevent the Confederacy from arriving first, the exact location was kept secret until the fleet left Hampton Roads on October 29, 1861.

The Port Royal Expedition was planned as a joint Army-Navy operation. The Navy flotilla of 17 warships carrying between 120-155 guns, 25 ships transporting coal, and 33 transport vessels with men, supplies, 500 landing crafts, and ammunition, was under the command of Captain Samuel Frances DuPont. The military, consisting of 1300 Army and Marine troops, 1500 horses, and a 1000 men labor force made up of free Blacks, were commanded by General Thomas W. Sherman. (Note: there seems to be no agreement on the above figures among historians.)

With calm waters, the fleet maintained its formation 36 hours behind DuPont's *Wabash*—a large 44-gun warship. The calm, however, was not to last and high seas caused twenty vessels to either return to Hampton Roads or seek safety closer to land. On the last day of October, the winds relented and there were smooth seas again, but it proved to be the calm before the storm.

As the fleet passed Cape Hatteras into South Carolina water, it was met by a hurricane-strength storm. On DuPont's orders, all captains shortened sails and pointed their bows into the wind to ride it out. On November 2, DuPont arose and scanned the horizon. Writing his wife, Sophie, he said, "This morning the fleet was nowhere." But as the hours passed, ships, one-by-one, came limping in to form alongside the comforting bulk of the *Wabash*. By November 4, twenty-five ships anchored off Port Royal Sound.

The newly created Confederate Government knew that a blockade of its ports was imminent. In May 1861, General P.G.T. Beauregard of the Confederate States Army examined the whole coast of South Carolina and mapped out plans for a coastal defense. Shortly after his inspection of Hilton Head Island on May 16, he issued the following report to Governor Francis W. Pickens:

I am of the opinion that the entrance to the magnificent and important harbor of Port Royal can be effectually protected by two strong works on Bay Point and Hilton Head, on each side of the entrance, and the steel-clad floating battery moored half way between the two, all armed with the heaviest rifled guns that can be made.

While Beauregard's request for the heaviest rifled guns that could be made and a floating battery never materialized, construction of the forts began in July. When the log and earthen fort on Bay Point across the sound from Hilton Head was completed, it was named in Beauregard's honor.

The larger and more important fort on Hilton Head Island was built under the direction of Major Frances Lee, an architect from Charleston. To build this fort, slaves from the island were put to work hauling palmetto logs, digging trenches, erecting a power magazine and constructing gun emplacements. By September, Fort Walker, named in honor of the Confederate Secretary of War, L.P. Walker, was operational. (After the battle, upon seeing the fort up close, DuPont remarked, "The works are most scientifically constructed and there is nothing like Walker on the Potomac.")

At the time of the attack, Fort Walker mounted 23 guns—mostly obsolete 32-pounders. Fort Beauregard contained 18 similar pieces of artillery. The Confederate garrisons, numbering about 2,400 men, were commanded by General Thomas Drayton, who happened to own a plantation on the island. And in the true spirit of "brother against brother," Thomas's brother, Percival Drayton, commanded the Union's *Pocahontas* under DuPont. Delayed by the storm, Percival arrived shortly before noon, and placing his ship unusually close, fired flanking shots into Fort Walker.

As with every other Southern port, the rebels had removed all navigational aids. So before the fleet could attack, the coast survey steamer *Vixen*, with Charles Boutelle, a coastal survey expert, and Charles Davis of DuPont's staff, sounded the channel and placed marker buoys. Simultaneously, four gunboats conducting a reconnaissance of the two forts entered the sound. (The planned joint Army-Navy attack never transpired because ships carrying needed ammunition and landing craft were either delayed or lost due to the storm.)

Not long into the sound, three tugs and a river boat steamer, under the command of Confederate Commodore Josiah Tattnall, appeared from Skull Creek. After exchanging a few rounds of fire, the four vessels made a hasty retreat.

On November 5, with the channel marked and the noon-high tide, DuPont decided on a head-on attack of Fort Walker. But the buoy markers set by Boutelle and Davis had come adrift, and both the *Wabash* and the *Susquehanna* ran aground on one of the sandbars hidden by the high tide. By the time the *Wabash* was free, it was too late in the day to continue.

Wednesday, November 6 dawned with fair skies, but the wind created unpredictable tides, so the attack was aborted. But the delay in fighting gave Charles Davis time to mull over the shot pattern of the forts he observed when being fired upon on November 4. By the next morning, Davis realized the northern face of Fort Walker contained no canon and would be most vulnerable.

Still in his nightclothes, Davis rushed into DuPont's cabin to present his plan of attack that called for two columns of ships to move in the sound. The main column, made up of the nine larger and heaviest ships, would face Fort Walker. The second column would face Fort Beauregard. As the ships entered the sound, they would simultaneously fire on both strongholds. Once two miles into the sound, the main column of gunboats would make an oval-like maneuver by turning west and heading back past Fort Walker. Then they would fire on the fort at close range until reaching the mouth of the sound, where they would turn about to retrace the oval course. (Nine vessels were to comprise the main column, yet all but three broke off and dropped anchor inside the sound, leaving only the *Wabash, Susquehanna* and *Bienville* to actually carry out the oval maneuver.) The small warships would prevent Tattnall from attacking from Skull Creek and fire into the unarmed northern face of Fort Walker. The shelling, and the oval attack, would continue until the forts were surrendered or abandoned.

A reporter from Harper's Weekly described the battle this way:

At about twenty minutes to eleven o'clock the Wabash commenced operations on Hilton Head battery in earnest...The noise was terrific, while the bursting of shells was terrible as it was destructive. I counted no less than forty shells bursting at one time...In addition to this, the Susquehanna *with her tremendous battery, aided by the* Bienville, *the* Pawnee *and a half dozen smaller gunboats, was making the air brown with sand, while the blue smoke of the explosions went to make up a most magnificent sight...The rebels replied with seven guns which were working splendidly, and from appearances they did considerable execution.*

At half past eleven the Wabash *and her consorts drew near the Hilton Head battery again, the rebels keeping up a brisk fire upon them as they approached...At ten minutes before twelve o'clock again the ships were enveloped in a dense cloud of white smoke, and in a few seconds shells were bursting into the battery in a splendid manner. The sand was flying in every direction and it seemed impossible that anyone who was within the walls of the battery could be saved from death. The rebels worked only two guns, I will give them the credit that they worked them beautifully. In just twenty minutes over two hundred shells burst over their heads and in the works...The rebel battery is badly damaged and the houses and tents bear the marks of shells...It looks as if there is a stampede in the rebel camp.*

In fact, the fort itself had been damaged little, and only ten rebels were killed with about twenty or so wounded, but their guns were useless.

Sometime after 1:00 P.M., the *Wabash, Susquehanna* and *Bienville* completed their third deadly oval. General Thomas Drayton ordered a retreat—there was no actual surrender of Port Royal. Commander John Gills of the Seminole went ashore, walked along the top of Fort Walker's earthen walls, then disappeared. A few minutes later he emerged atop the Pope family mansion where he ran the Stars and Stripes up the towering flag pole. Cheers erupted from the fleets, and brass bands on several ships began playing *The Star-Spangled Banner*.

1.—BATTLE OF THE UNION FLEET WITH FORTS WALKER AND BEAUREGARD. 2.—HOISTING THE STARS AND STRIPES OVER FORT WALKER. FROM WAR-TIME SKETCHES.

Because General Sherman could not land his troops until 4:00 P.M., the Southern soldiers were able to successfully withdraw to the mainland. For generations, freemen on the Sea Islands remembered November 7 as the "Day of the Big Gun Shoot." Today, the remains of Fort Walker, renamed Fort Wells in honor of the Secretary of the Union Navy Gideon Wells, are located on Port Royal Plantation.[iii]

Hilton Head Island was occupied by the Union from November 7, 1861 until January 14, 1868. As the Department of the South of the United States Army, the island became a coal-refueling and maintenance facility for blockade ships, a base that cared for the sick and wounded, and a prisoner of war site. The installation contained almost 50,000 people (more than what live on the island today) with two weekly newspapers, four hotels, a string of saloons, numerous shops along "Robber's Row"—which charged soldiers and sailors outrageous prices, hence the name—a theater, and a bakery.

Despite the success of the Port Royal Expedition, it can also be seen as a lapse of strategic planning. The forces and mission given to General Thomas Sherman were adequate only for holding the immediate objective of Port Royal with little consideration of pushing inland from the Atlantic Coast. Any such advance would have forced the Confederacy to fight a three-front war: in Virginia; along the Mississippi; and, if done, at Charleston and Savannah. According to Percival Drayton of the Pawnee, it was "A great pity...so far as operating against the enemy goes."

Union soldiers and sailors who died at Port Royal were buried at the cemetery on Union Cemetery Road, but were moved to the Beaufort National Cemetery shortly after the war. Today, the cemetery on Union Cemetery Road is a Gullah cemetery.

Related YouTube video:
"Battle of Port Royal Fiber Optic Exhibit"

Mitchelville, an Experiment in Citizenship

The conquest of Port Royal and the surrounding areas by the Union was so swift that planters abandoned most of their property and headed inland. Consequently, within a few days, nearly ten thousand slaves were abandoned on Sea Island Plantations. Because these "freed" slaves were viewed by the government as abandoned property, or contraband of war, they were placed under the jurisdiction of the U. S. Department of Treasury.

From the very beginning, housing and caring for freedmen was a problem. First, freedmen were given tents, and then "commodious barracks" were built. These long, white wooden structures, located within the Union camps, were "crowded [with] young and old, male and female, without respect either to quality or quantity...becom[ing] a sort of...half stye, half brothel." Relationships between freedmen and soldiers also proved troubling. Both competed for rations and some troops reverted to stealing from ex-slaves. There was widespread racism on the part of soldiers, who were all too often guilty of sexually assaulting black women and girls. "Women were held as the legitimate prey of lust, and as they have been taught it was a crime to resist a white man."

It soon became apparent that "some wholesome changes" were needed to allow freedmen to have "more comfort and freedom for improvement." The person who would be responsible for these changes was General O. M. Mitchel, who took command of the Department of the South in September 1862. The "experiment in citizenship" was radically different from other refugee camps located at Beaufort, Bay Point and Otter Island.

Before his death from malaria only four months after arriving, Mitchel issued the following military order:

I. All lands now set apart for the colored population, near Hilton Head, are declared to constitute a village. * Only freedmen and colored persons residing or sojourning within the territory of the village shall be deemed and considered inhabitants.

(*The village would be named Mitchelville shortly after Mitchel's death.)

II. The village shall be divided into districts, as nearly equal in population as practicable, for the election of councilmen, sanitary and police regulations, and the general government for the people residing therein.

III. The government shall consist of a Supervisor and Treasurer...assisted by a councilman from each council district, to be elected by the people, who shall also, at the same time, choose a Recorder and Marshal.

IV. The Supervisor and Councilmen shall constitute the Council of Administration, with the Recorder as Secretary.

V. The Council of Administration shall have power to: establish schools for the education of children and other persons; prevent and punish vagrancy, idleness and crime; punish licentiousness, drunkenness, offenses against public decency and good order, and petty violation of the rights of property and person; require due observance of the Lord's Day; collect fines and penalties; punish offenses against village ordinances; settle and determine disputes concerning claims for wages, personal property, and controversies between debtor and creditor; levy and collect taxes to defray the expenses of government, and for the support of schools; lay out, regulate and clean the streets; establish wholesale sanitary regulations for the prevention of disease; and appoint officers, places and times for the holding of elections.

Hilton Head Island will be divided into school districts...In each district there shall be one School Commissioner ... Every child, between the ages of six and fifteen years, residing within the limits of such school districts, shall attend school daily, while they are in session, exception only in the cases of sickness ... And the parents and guardians will be held responsible that said children so attend school, under the penalty of being punished.

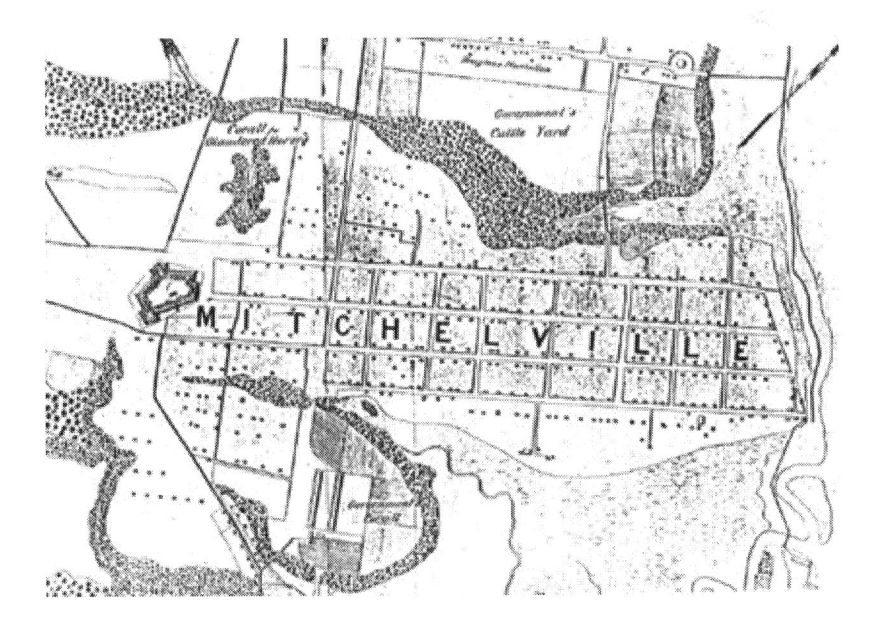

A map of Mitchelville of the time clearly shows the 165-acre village was laid out with four main streets and upwards to 100 houses on quarter acre lots. The village ran from Port Royal Sound to where Fort Howell would be constructed in 1864.

Houses were simple, two-room structures made of wood planks (provided by Union saw mills) or tabby.

It was reported that upwards to one thousand blacks were employed by the military. Freedmen worked as laborers and skilled craftsmen in the camp, construction sites, docks, plantations and hospitals. More importantly, many freedmen were eager to try their hands at life in the world, with many working for officers with most desirable financial results on their part. Women, in addition to paid plantation work, washed clothes for officers and soldiers, made cakes and pies for sale, and sold any surplus potatoes, turnips and cabbages they grew. Many freedmen, after Emancipation arrived, began buying confiscated land from the government with the money they earned and saved. Freedmen on Hilton Head were never given any free land by the government.

With Mitchelville being separated from the Union camp by Fish Haul Creek, it appears the residents were truly left to run their own affairs. In the archives of the American Missionary Association (A.M.A), is a letter written just a few days before the Union army left the island in January 7, 1867 that reads:

There are several large plantations upon which are small settlements, but the greater part of the colored population of the island are located a short distance from Hilton Head [meaning the old military base] *at a place called Mitchelville . . . It is an incorporated town, regularly laid out in streets and squares. About 1500 inhabitants, not a single white person. There are three churches - two Baptist, one Methodist, two schools which are taught by A.M.A. teachers.*

By all accounts, Mitchelville was a successful experiment with emancipation and citizenship. However, Mitchelville suffered the fate many small towns do today when the main employer moves their operations overseas. When the military evacuated the island in January 1868, the residents faced unemployment and turned to subsistence farming to survive. Some formed "collectives" where they rented land from the government, and many purchased land which some descendants still occupy today.

"In 2005, a diverse group of Hilton Head Island citizens joined forces to preserve, protect and promote the heritage of Mitchelville, America's first post-Civil War settlement for freed slaves ... The mission is to replicate, preserve, and sustain a historically significant site and to educate the public about the sacrifice, resilience and perseverance of the freedmen of Mitchelville and to share the story of how these brave men and women planted strong and enduring familial roots for generations of future African-Americans."(From the Mitchelville Preservation Project web site. Mitchelville Freedom Park is part of Fish Haul Creek Park at the end of 229 Beach City Rd)

Related YouTube video:
"Voices of the Civil War Episode 9: "Port Royal Experiment"

Fort Howell

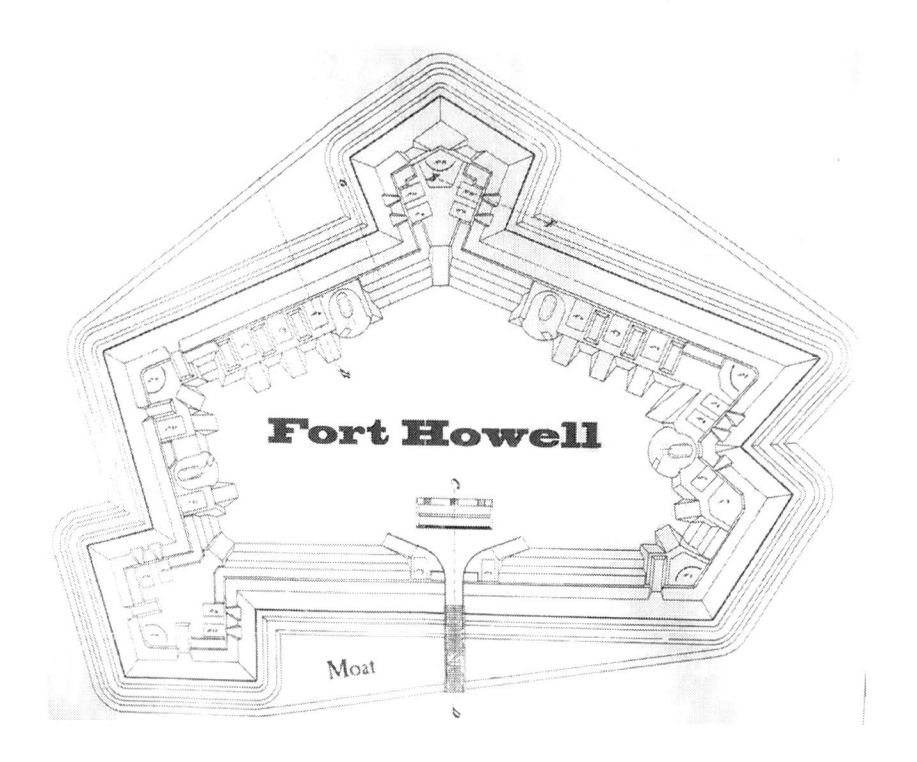

Fort Howell is a Civil War earthwork fortification constructed by the United States Army in 1864. It is located near the intersection of Beach City Road and Dillon, right across from Hilton Head Airport. Today the fort is owned by the Hilton Head Island Land Trust, Inc., a non-profit organization whose goal is to protect and preserve it in perpetuity.

The fort was constructed from late August or early September to late November 1864 by the 32nd United States Colored Infantry and the 144th New York Infantry—regiments belonging to the Hilton Head District, Department of the South, United States Army.

Fort Howell, a pentagonal enclosure constructed of built-up earth, is quite visible despite natural erosion and the growth of trees and other vegetation over a period of almost 150 years. (Ironically, the trees and vegetation help to prevent erosion of the walls.) Its construction is typical of earthen Civil War fortifications, but the size, sophistication of design, and physical integrity are all exceptional in the context of surviving Civil War fortifications in South Carolina. Most large earthwork structures, whether constructed by Federal or Confederate troops, have much less integrity than Fort Howell does.

*　　*　　*

Throughout the spring and summer of 1864, infantry, artillery, and cavalry units were transferred from coastal South Carolina, Georgia, and Florida to support the massive campaigns underway in northern Virginia and northern Georgia.

At the end of April, Colonel William W.H. Davis, commanding the Hilton Head District at the time (consisting of Hilton Head and St. Helena Islands in South Carolina and Fort Pulaski and Tybee Island in Georgia), estimated that he needed at least 3,000 men to defend Hilton Head Island alone. He commented, "I do not believe the enemy will attempt anything beyond raids, but there should be preparations for a more serious attack."

On August 17, 1864, then commander of Department of the South, General John G. Foster, ordered the design and construction of three new earthworks on the island. There were listed as: 1. a large earthwork bastion to be added to the 1862 earthen lines running from northeast to southwest and to be named Fort Sherman (in today's Port Royal Plantation); 2. a new pentagonal earthwork at the southern end of the freedmen's village of Mitchellville to be named Fort Howell; and 3. the completion of the new earthwork on the southwestern shore of the island, to be named Battery Holbrook (located in today's Spanish Wells plantation).

Fort Howell was intended to defend the two main roads leading to Mitchelville and other nearby roads leading to the Hilton Head District Port Royal military installation.

Fatigue details, (a group of soldiers ordered to perform menial, nonmilitary tasks) from the 32nd United States Colored Infantry, did most of the construction from late August or early September to mid-October 1864, using shovels, spades, picks, and axes. The 32nd Infantry numbered approximately 500 officers and men, with white commissioned officers and black noncommissioned officers and other enlisted men.

Work on the fort was slowed and complicated for two reasons. First was its officers' apparent reluctance to assign sufficient men to the task, and second, its soldiers' apparent reluctance toward or inability to perform the hard labor necessary to complete it. It was common for Federal commanders to assign their black units to fatigue duty, and especially to employ them to build or improve field fortifications. In this way they could "save" their white units for combat. By mid-October the 32nd United States Colored Infantry was split up, with its companies ordered to various points on Hilton Head Island and elsewhere in the Department of the South. Fatigue details from the 144th New York (white)Infantry completed the fort from mid-October to late November 1864.

* * *

Fort Howell is one of the most intact and best-preserved Civil War field fortifications in South Carolina and is a fine example of a sophisticated Federal earthwork. Its method of construction—built-up earth, reinforced by wooden timbers and supplemented by wooden platforms as necessary—was a change from earlier brick and stone masonry forts. The need for such modification was the result of advances in weaponry that occurred as the Civil War approached. Rifled cannons came into use, and with their increased range, power, and accuracy over the previous smoothbore cannons, they could easily breach the older style masonry fort walls. The dirt walls of the Civil War earthen fort could better absorb incoming rifled field artillery shells and protect the men and weapons inside the fort.

Artillery during this period was either smoothbore or rifled (spiral grooves cut in the inner surface of the gun barrel to give the round a rotatory motion and thus a more precise trajectory), with both types primarily muzzle-loading. It is not known what guns, if any, were actually mounted in the fort, but it was designed to hold as many as 27 guns.

Fort Howell never saw action, for by the time it was completed near the end of 1864, the Confederate Department of South Carolina, Georgia, and Florida lacked the forces to offer much of a significant threat to the Federal presence on Hilton Head Island.

A major misconception about the fort is that it once was a wooden structure. When visiting, what one will see is an earthwork fortification that had walls 26 feet in height. Also, at the time of its construction, there were no trees on or near the fort—just cotton fields surrounded the area.

* * *

On September 26, 1864, the fort was named in honor of General Joshua Blackwood Howell of Pennsylvania who briefly commanded the Hilton Head District, Department of the South, earlier that year. He helped organize and was the first colonel of the 85th Pennsylvania Infantry. Howell commanded his regiment in Virginia for the first months of the war, then commanded a brigade in the Army of the Potomac during the Peninsular Campaign of March-May 1862.

During the Siege of Charleston, as a result of being wounded in action at Battery Wagner in August 1863, Howell was assigned command of the Hilton Head District from February 6 to April 26, 1864. His brigade was then transferred to Virginia, and while commanding a division near Petersburg, his horse fell on him on September 12, 1864. Howell died from his injuries two days later.

* * *

Admission to Fort Howell is free and the site is open daily from dawn to dusk. It takes about 15-20 minutes to cover all the grounds. The Hilton Head Island Trust has erected interpretive markers; an enclosed, shaded, kiosk with inscriptions containing facts related to the fort; a time-period Union flag; and metal sculptures by local artist, Mary Ann Browning Ford, displaying some of the individuals who were important to the fort's history.

Related YouTube video:
"African American Civil War Infantry honored at Fort Howell"

Fort Mitchel

Fort Mitchel is a Civil War earthwork fortification on a 3.27-acre site at 65 Skull Creek Drive in Hilton Head Plantation adjacent to Old Fort Pub. The fort was constructed in late November 1861 by the Department of the South, United States Army, and was part of the Federal defenses of Hilton Head Island. Intended to protect the Skull Creek approaches to the coaling station and ship maintenance facilities about a mile to the northeast, it was built in half-moon shaped called a lunette on a bluff situated about fifteen feet above Skull Creek. Fort Mitchel is named for Major General Ormsby MacKnight Mitchel, who took command of the Department of the South in September 1862, and briefly commanded forces stationed here before his death due to yellow fever in October 1862. It also represents a rare example of a large semi-permanent Federal field fortification in the South Carolina Lowcountry. The period of significance, 1862-1864, spans the period from its construction until its abandonment by Union forces.

A gate pass is required to access the community where Fort Mitchel is located, but can be easily picked up on site at the small entrance guard station, free of charge. While Fort Mitchel clearly isn't a well-preserved relic of the Civil War, it's nonetheless one of Hilton Head Island's most scenic.

Related YouTube video:
"Fort Mitchel, Hilton Head Island SC"

Years of Isolation

Eighty years of isolation would follow the Union's withdrawal from the island in 1868. The freedmen who remained survived by practicing subsistence farming, hunting, fishing, and oystering. Gone were plantation houses and cotton fields, thus allowing native plants, animals and trees to regain their natural glory. This was particularly true in the south Sea Pines half of the island, with Gullah residents living in ten autonomous neighborhoods on the island's northern end.

In 1872, the Federal government began the process of returning land lost during the war to plantations owner; however, the process was fraught with numerous hurdles. To reclaim confiscated land, a family had to prove ownership, but during Sherman's march to the sea, the county seat holding land records was destroyed. If ownership was established, back taxes, interest, and penalties had to be paid, but many previous owners had lost everything during the war and were living a life of financial hardship. Also, land the government sold to freedmen was protected and was not redeemable. (It is true that previous owners were reimbursed by the government for this land, but it was nowhere near its true value.)

Those families who were able to reclaim their land on the island (the Elliots, Lawtons, Matthews, Drayton, Popes, and Baynards), found it no longer profitable. Under the control of the Freedmen's Bureau, owners were required to pay freedmen for their labor and were limited in terms of how much they could charge for rent. To make matters worse, there was little demand for Sea Island cotton, and freedmen, who no longer wanted to labor on plantations, found work in area phosphate mines and fertilizer production facilities.

Consequently, by the 1880s, reclaimed land was being sold at rock-bottom prices to freedmen and wealthy outsiders.

One group that did climb into boats and venture to the island to take advantage of the inexpensive land were hunters. The first to arrive were the members of the Beaufort Gun Club in the 1880s. They bought the Leamington and Hill plantations and hunted their 1,770 acres until 1918.

*   *   *

After the devastation of the Civil War, a few enterprising capitalists found great wealth in the textile manufacturing business in North Carolina. And while much of their Southern way of life had been destroyed, hunting was one Southern pastime they could still enjoy. But cotton was in their blood, and believing Sea Island cotton could again be grown on Hilton Head, they formed the Hilton Head Agricultural Company.

The company, made up of twenty-six charter stockholders, purchased the Beaufort Gun Club land with three main objectives: 1) Grow, gin and sell cotton, as well as, raise, sell, or trade horses, cattle and other livestock; 2) Buy, hold, and sell real estate; 3) Sell merchandise and trade goods. Hunting was at first seen only as a perk in becoming a shareholder. By the 1920s, though, the boll weevil infestation transformed the "Agricultural Company" into a full-fledge hunting club.

At the company's formation, stockholders represented the cotton-mill elite and the pillars of their communities. Members came from the towns of Gastonia, Clover, and Chattanooga, and had separate week-long hunts. Only during the Christmas hunt was there any mixing of members. Over time, the number of stockholders would be increased to forty-four, and members grew more diverse to include doctors, dentists, building contractors, car dealers, etc. And despite being a male fraternity, over-drinking and foul language were discouraged.

The club property was a mix of clear and wild land to ensure a variety of sporting activity. Generally, hunters were dropped off at various points to encircle three sides of an area, and then game would be driven to them by Jake Brown and his dogs. After the hunt, Jake would hang up the kill, clean the carcasses, and move them to the meat house.

Jake, a Gullah native, was an integral part of the company for thirty-three years. He was "master of the hounds" and deer driver, and knew every game trail and thicket on the island. Because Jake was held in such high regard by the Gullah community, he served as the intermediate between the hunters and the locals. Today, Jake's grave can be found in Union Cemetery and reads:

Jake Brown
May 5, 1884—May 6, 1950
Care Taker & Driver
Hilton Head Agricultural Co.
1917—1950

Over time, the club established several rituals and antics. The blood of a deer would be smudged on the face of the hunter who got his first kill. Those hunters who shot but missed their target had their shirt tails cut and mounted on the wall for all to see. But a member could regain his pride by climbing onto and riding "Charlie YW," an ox owned by a local preacher.

Hearing tales about how fabulous the hunting was on the island, several wealthy Northerners began buying up land for a dollar or two an acre. In 1889, the New York shipping baron, William P. Clyde, who had been stationed on the island during the Civil War, bought 9,000 acres. His island domain included Honey Horn Plantation, the only surviving plantation house on the island, which he restored and made his hunting-vacation lodge. (Honey Horn was built as "Hanahan" Plantation but was linguistically transformed by the Gullah language.)

After a short time, Clyde sold his land to another wealthy New Yorker, Roy Rainey. During the 1920s, Rainey came to own half the island, but with the 1929 stock market crash, was forced to sell. The New York financiers, Alfred L. Loomis and Landon K. Thorne, who bought Rainey's half of the island, soon controlled two-thirds of the island. Like Clyde and Rainey before them, Thorne and Loomis made Honey Horn their headquarters and entertained and hunted in grand style.

Another rich Northerner, William L. Hurley, who owned and operated one the nation's first department store chains, built his estate on the west side of Broad Creek. Hurley is remembered for ferrying the first automobile to the island. It was also during the 1890s that the Hudsons, Toomers, and Maggionis opened oystering, shrimping and seafood packing businesses to meet the growing demand for seafood on the East Coast.

*   *   *

Three times during this period, the Federal government returned to the island for military purposes. In 1897, during the Spanish-American War, the Department of the Army authorized Edmund Zalinski, a Polish-born American soldier and military engineer, to build his steam or Zalinski dynamite gun on the island. A steam generator was used to compress air into storage reservoirs. When the air was released, the cannon propelled a seven-foot long projectile filled with dynamite over three miles. While fired over one hundred times, it was never used in battle and was disassembled in 1902. Today, the concrete emplacements are still visible at Port Royal Plantation and can be seen on the "Forts of Port Royal" tour conducted by the Coastal Discovery Museum.

During World War I, troops were stationed at Coggins Point, near Fort Walker (Port Royal Plantation), to keep a lookout for enemy submarines that might be trying to attack the East Coast. And then in the late 1930s, Marines built a base on the old Leamington Lighthouse Reservation. It was used throughout World War II as a training camp for anti-aircraft units and defense battalions. The Marines would be the ones to pave the first road on the island. It ran from the island's ferry landing to Camp McDougal near Leamington and Palmetto Dunes. (Today, it is William Hilton Parkway.) Soon after the war, the base was closed and the land sold to the

Hilton Head Agricultural Company. In the 1980s the lighthouse became a landmark on the Arthur Hills Golf Course within the Palmetto Dunes Resort.

*   *   *

This period of isolation is referred to by the Gullah community as "before the bridge." Until the late 1920s, sailboats were the primary means of transportation to and from the Island. In the 1930s, passenger ferries ran between Savannah and Beaufort, stopping at Daufuskie and Hilton Head Islands. Also in the 1930s, Charlie Simmons, known as "Mr. Transportation" among the local community, bought the first locally owned motorboat. For twenty-five years, Simmons took people, mail, produce, livestock, and anything else from Hilton Head to Savannah and back. In 1953, Mose Hudson began operating a state-run ferry to Hilton Head. It crossed Skull Creek five times a day until 1956 when the first bridge to the island was built.

Related YouTube video:
"Hilton Head History - the Hilton Head Agricultural Society"

"The Hilton Head Agricultural Society maintained hunting grounds mid-island from 1917-1967. This video contains footage shot during the 1950s, some of which was shot from the plane of hunt club member Dr. John Quickel. Music by Lowcountry Boil."

Hilton Head Monthly
Published on Oct 25, 2012

The African-American in the video is Jake Brown.

Lowcountry Boil Bluegrass Band performs around the island and Bluffton. They are always a fun time with great songs.

Related YouTube videos:
"Lowcountry Boil Christmas Special Chapter Two"
"Lowcountry Boil Band MUDD."

The author

While it was true enslaved Africans had some inherited resistance to tropical diseases, their masters were extremely vulnerable. Because of this, white planters lived miles away from their rice and cotton fields, and visited their plantations only between March and October. A white manager, or overseer, would be in charge of day-to-day operations, and even then, he might delegate that responsibility to a trusted slave working as foreman or "driver." Thus, the coastal and island enslaved Africans had little contact with Whites, which allowed them to blend together the various African tribal traditions to form their own Gullah language, rituals, customs, religion, music, crafts and diet. The task system of labor would also play an instrumental part in this process.

In 1787, the South Carolina legislature closed the slave trade, but out of fear created by the newly adopted U.S. Constitution banning the slave trade in 1820, the law was reversed. The final and feverish period of the slave trade lasted from 1804-1808 with forty thousand new African immigrants being brought to South Carolina. These "new" slaves were mainly assigned to work on rice and Sea Island cotton plantations. The majority of these slaves were natives of the Congo-Angola region of Africa, and it is believed the term "Gullah" derived from Angola or "N'gulla" – as it would have been phonetically spoken. It would be this final group that brought a renewed infusion of African traditions, words, skills, and religious beliefs to most strongly impact the development of the Gullah language and culture. As noted earlier, most plantation owners seldom went to their rice or cotton plantations; instead, they delegated the running of the operations to overseers. This, combined with the task system which encouraged family, religious, and community activities, enabled slaves to carry on their African-derived customs and practices without fear of interference.

Out of a need to communicate with one another came their creole Gullah language. Creole is the name used for a language that has evolved from the mixture of one or more languages and has become the first language of the group. As a creole language, Gullah began as a pidgin, a simplified speech used for communication among people of different languages. The pidgin likely began in outdoor prison-like enclosures where captives were held before being loaded onto slave ships. As pidgin became the main form of communication, the processes of linguistic evolution took over to produce a complete language. Although many Gullah words are derived from English, Gullah is decidedly not a dialect of English. Gullah is recognized by linguists as a separate language distinguished from English by mutual unintelligibility, i.e., native speakers of only Gullah or only English would not be able to understand one another. And once a common language had been created, the great diversity of cultures, traditions, languages, and religions were mixed and fused together, and a new hybrid African culture, called Gullah, emerged.

Throughout the Gullah Corridor, extended families of common ancestral relationships are more common than nuclear families with no blood ties. Marriages may be common-law with the consent of the families involved rather than being sanctioned by the state or a religious body. Women are the most stabilizing members of the household and are primarily in charge of upbringing, religious training, and passing on family lore. Generally, intergenerational family members live in clusters of homes on compounds established on land purchased after Emancipation. Through these multi-family communities, the web of kinship assures no one goes hungry, and there are funds for weddings and funerals.

The distinctiveness of Gullah culture is clearly defined through a variety of artistic and craft traditions such as metalworking, quilting, basketry, net making, woodcarving, music, and folklore. Gullah people have a rich tradition of oral literature and history including legends, folktales, stories, and accounts of supernatural events such as spiritual attacks by hags and other evil entities. Some elements of Gullah culture have been popularized through the creative arts in such works as George Gershwin's folk opera *Porgy and Bess* (1934). Generations of Americans have delighted in *The Uncle Remus tales. The Uncle Remus* stories were animal trickster tales in which animals took on human emotions and behaviors. While there is debate over the specific African, European, or American Indian sources for these tales, they were a coherent body of oral literature, which is a distinctly Gullah creation. The tales usually portrayed weak characters outwitting the strong and fostered the idea of freedom within the confines of slavery. Gullah children learned many lessons from these stories, not the least of which were derived from allegories of the manipulation of power by the weak as well as the strong.

Among the most readily identifiable Gullah products are coiled sea grass baskets. Early baskets were made for various practical agricultural and domestic uses in the plantation economy and were generally made by men or elders who were unable to work in the fields. Basketry and other crafts were part of the bartering system and became another source of income for economic survival in the lean years immediately following the Civil War. In the 1970s, Gregory K. Day, a cultural anthropologist, collected examples of Sea Islands basketry for the Smithsonian to document the survival of

African traditions in contemporary African American life. Within a few years, sweetgrass baskets were featured in museums and galleries around the world. During the late 20th century and continuing into the present, basketmaking became a focal point for dynamic change and evolution in Gullah culture, as basket makers continue to develop new styles and forms to meet a growing demand for their work. (While on the island, one can see how baskets are made Coastal Discovery Museum, 70 Honey Horn Drive Hilton Head Island Hilton Head Island, SC 29926.)

Plantation owners originally built Praise Houses as a means of social control, but with the end of slavery, they became the central place for spiritual guidance and group leadership. Until the late 1960s, Praise Houses were strategically located across the island, but today there are no Praise Houses left standing on Hilton Head. In fact, with the exception of the Church of Christ, Gullah church services reflect mainstream Black churches. Music, performed by a choir and accompanied by piano, organ, and drums, etc., is expected to inspire the pastor whose sermon is expected to inspire the souls of members until the next Sunday.

During the era of Praise Houses, in order to articulate their spiritual lives, the Gullah often participated in the "shout." The tradition of the shout consists of call-and-response singing and rhythmic dance movements in a counterclockwise circle. Shouters progress around the circle with a shuffling movement wherein feet are never crossed and never leave the ground. In 1872, Charles Stearns described the shout: "A ring of singers is formed in an open space in the room, and they, without holding on to each other's hands, walk slowly around and around in a circle … They then utter a kind of melodious chant, which gradually increases in strength, and in noise, until it fairly shakes the house, and it can be heard for a long distance ..." The word shout is thought to be derived from saut, a West African word of Arabic origin that describes an Islamic religious movement performed to exhaustion.

The Gullah believe in the dual nature of the soul and spirit. In death, one's soul returns to God but the spirit remains on earth and is involved in the daily affairs of its living descendants. For example, a spirit will visit a family member on various occasions to advise or counsel him or her through spiritual means. While adhering to Christian doctrine, many Gullah continue to hold traditional African beliefs. Witchcraft, which they call *wudu, wanga, joso, or juju,* is one example. Some Gullah believe that witches can cast a spell by putting powerful herbs or roots under a person's pillow or at a place where he or she usually walks.

This chapter has been expanded into my short book, *Gullah Culture: 1670 to 1950*. It is available from both Amazon and Barnes & Noble as an eBook, and as a paperback from Amazon. Royalties from my books are donated to nonprofit organizations.

Related YouTube video:
"Gullah Traditions of the South Carolina Coast"

Two Decades of Change

After World War II, Hilton Head Island was covered with virgin timber which attracted people in the lumbering business. Fred C. Hack, who scouted properties for lumber companies, made a trip to the island in 1949. Upon discovering 8,000 acres of timber on the southern third of the island, he sought out the owners—Loomis and Thorne. Hack hoped they would be receptive to selling the rights to the timber, but soon discovered they were only interested in selling the land outright.

Lacking the money to buy the land himself, Hack returned home to Hinesville, Georgia and asked Joseph B. Fraser, of the Fraser Lumber Company, to go in with him. Fraser agreed and became principle stockholder in the Hilton Head Company. Other investors included Fraser's father-in-law C. C. Stebbins, and longtime business friend, Olin T. McIntosh. Soon after the acquisition, Fraser, a general in the National Guard, was sent to South Korea. While away, Hack and McIntosh purchased the rest of the Loomis—Thorne land and called their new company Honey Horn Plantation. Between the Hilton Head and Honey Horn Plantation companies, they own most of the island.

Under the direction of the Fraser Lumber Company, three lumber mills were set up. By 1952, the timber operation ended and the owners turned their attention to developing Hilton Head into a seaside resort. Hack, who had some experience in development, moved his family to Honey Horn Plantation and took charge of the next phase of operations.

Before building could realistically begin, two hurdles had to be overcome. The first was to convince the Palmetto Electric Cooperative to bring electricity to the island in 1951. The second, with the help of J. Wilton Graves, a state legislator from Beaufort County, was to convince the state government to authorize ferry operations to and from the island in 1953. (Graves would also play an instrumental role in getting the state to permit the construction of the bridge in 1956.)

After the bridge's construction, it was apparent people would come to the island, but how the island paradise would be developed remained in question. Could the wide beaches, rolling dunes, lush foliage and rich wildlife—in and out of water—be protected from destruction? This was a time in the country when growth was seen as good, with little or no regard given to the natural environment. And what would be the fate of the Gullah residences scattered across the island? Since the Civil War, they had built stable and self-sustaining communities.

The individual who set the tone of how the island would be developed was Charles E. Fraser, son of General Fraser. While at Yale, Fraser had taken a land-use planning class from Myers McDougal, author of *Property, Wealth, Land: Allocation, Planning and Development*. Its overriding theme was that property ought to be planned, and when it is not, the results can be destructive.

After graduation, Fraser traveled from Cape Cod to Key West seeking out developers of resort/retiree/vacation communities to study their concepts and techniques, but found there were no prototypes for the kind of resort he wanted to build. Breaking with conventional wisdom, Fraser invented an approach to private development that created a new kind of resort in purpose, architecture and design, and environmental sensitivity. The guiding principles on which he would build his Sea Pines were: 1) Do not impose development on the environment, blend it in; 2) Create green space for privacy; 3) Keep density as low as profitably possible; 4) Create roads for beauty and efficiency, not just for transit; 5) Build no structure higher than five stories tall; 6) Cut down only those trees that are absolutely necessary; 7) Think always of enhancing the quality of life for those who would be residents of the island.

Fraser also decided he would make the whole community desirable rather than focusing solely on the beach. Unexpectedly, golf courses proved to be the most successful means of enhancing the interior of the island. They created extensive green space and water around which to build houses, and they could be threaded through less attractive land that would be virtually worthless without a tended green space in front of it. Also, golf transformed the island from just a summer beach vacation destination to a year-round resort.

These principles were not only at the heart of Fraser's Sea Pines, but became the overriding principles that guided nearly all plantation development on the island. Also, it helped that Fraser, Hack, and McIntosh owned most of the island and were able to impose construction standards on most non-plantation land deals. To further their control, the major plantations provided water and sewer services, police and fire protection, roads and other facilities, thus making them the unelected local government of the island.

This is not to give the impression that there was total agreement between the three men. Hack and McIntosh wanted to develop their property in the traditional beachfront manner--simple beach houses on rectangular lots. (And while they wanted to give full sway to the island's natural beauty and emphasize its historic past, in all likelihood, the island would have been doomed like many other southern coastal resorts.) Upon learning of Fraser's proposed concept of Sea Pines Plantation with Harbour Town, golf courses, and tennis courts with the intent of attracting affluent people who would stay for only a week at a time in condominiums, Hack and McIntosh were appalled. They were also slow to embrace Fraser's idea of a plantation system with ironclad control over residents when they built their vacation or retirement homes. These, and other differences, would cause Fraser to break with Hack and McIntosh in 1956 and go on to create his world class resort.

Fraser was committed to the idea of blending man's work into the natural environment. The style of a home to be built first took into account its natural setting, and then the buyer's ideas would be considered. Homes were to be modern with an emphasis on natural materials and finishes, and to be open to nature with patios, large windows and balconies. Styles such as the English Tudor, Spanish Adobe, French Provincial, Gothic Revival, log cabin, geodesic dome, and ranch house were flatly rejected. After 1965, even stock house plans of any type were rejected in favor of individually designed homes by Fraser's own staff of young architects. In 1986, more than eighty percent of the single-family homes had been custom built.

Hack's first venture into a planned community was his Port Royal Plantation begun in 1962 on the northeast heel of the island. It was 1,000 acres with three miles of beaches, lush woods, glistening lagoons and historic ruins from two wars. In Port Royal, owners came first, and design standards were not as demanding as those of Sea Pines. However, owners were still required to build tasteful homes of high standards on suburban-sized lots. Life in Port Royal was billed as a place insulated from the multiplying condominiums and the growing hordes of tourists flocking to Harbour Town.

Olin McIntosh would take a very different approach with his Spanish Wells Plantation. The McIntosh family were sailors and designed the Spanish Well Peninsula around boating and a 9-hole golf course. What made Spanish Wells unique was its secluded landscape with magnificent trees and sweeping views of Broad Creek and Calibogue Sound. Large, stately homes, set back from the road on one acre lots, allowed the peninsula's natural beauty to take center stage.

As a result of his changing attitudes, Hack began his Shipyard Plantation in 1970. This project was designed to compete permanent residents (compared to Sea Pines 65% absentee ownership), Hilton Head Plantation was the main force behind economic and political power moving from the south to the northern half of the island.

*   *   *

The sweeping changes brought by development drastically altered the way of life and traditions of the Gullah people. Although they owned less than twenty percent of the island, for one hundred years they had roamed freely gathering wood, hunting, and fishing which made possible their subsistence life style. But with development came limited access to the land they depended on for survival.

The majority of the Gullahs made the transition from subsistence farming to the newly created service industry catering to wealthy whites, but these new jobs made no significant change in their economic status. And certainly, the major loss by the Gullah community was their language as they assimilated into the new "plan-tation" society.

*   *   *

In 2002, Charles Fraser and his wife, Mary, were on a chartered 29-foot boat in the Turks and Caicos Islands when the stern exploded. The islands are an internally self-governing overseas territory of the United Kingdom. His wife suffered minor injuries, but Fraser was killed. His body was buried next to the Liberty Oak in Harbour Town.

Related YouTube video:
"The Story Of Hilton Head South Carolina"

Paradise Almost Lost

As the economy recovered in the late 1970s, a flood of condominiums were constructed on Hilton Head Island. Built by newcomers on land outside the control of plantation companies, the new buildings only needed to satisfy the minimum Beaufort County building codes and the loosely enforced state health regulations. In other words, these "outparcels" were built without any restraints on location, size, density, quality or aesthetics.

Yet, demand for condominiums was high because they were so much more affordable than single-family houses on expensive lots. These condominiums also appealed to individuals growing tired of driving to the island every day to work in one of the new service industries: fast and fine dining, grocery stores, house/condo cleaning, lawn care, retail stores, real estate, banks, construction, medical, schools, churches, and resort activities and entertainment. In 1972, there were 120 businesses with 3,000 employees; ten years later, there were 850 businesses with 9,500 employees.

As may be expected, retirees, who made up one-third of the island's population, were most distressed over the development. Many had moved to the island when it truly was "wild and pristine" and built expensive homes of great beauty. (Many homes were so stunning that the *Islander Magazine* featured one each month with floor plans, photos and stories about the owners.) The decision to move to the island, particularly during the early years, was not a decision made lightly. So what happened next probably was more than a bit shocking.

After seeing how Hack was unable to retain control of his Hilton Head Company during the financial crises of the 1970s, Charles Fraser introduced the idea of time-shares to the island in 1975 with hopes of saving his Sea Pines. This new population, buying access to a condominium for one week a year, were of a lower socioeconomic class than the "islanders," and had no reason to feel any commitment to the island beyond their own vacation enjoyment. Not only was there a jump in the number of substandard condominiums built to meet the growing time-share demand, but some developers began trucking in high-density, prefabricated units. Islanders soon dubbed them stack-a-shacks, with the most notorious ones being Hilton Head Four Seasons, Hilton Head Beach and Tennis Club, Sea Cabins, and the Spa on Port Royal Sound. Plantation owners also grew concerned—their business was based on selling the good life in an attractive setting, not one visually polluted by unimaginative structures.

At first, islanders had faith that plantation companies and citizen groups might prove successful in persuading Beaufort County officials into passing special land use ordinances to protect the island's special character. Their concerns, though, fell on deaf ears. Over one half of Beaufort County's operating budget came from Hilton Head taxes, and one of the stack-a-shack companies hired a Beaufort County Councilman as their attorney. Consequently, county officials refused to act, and the island was on the verge of going the way of other oceanfront resorts with its fragile ecosystem going with it.

Barrier island beaches, even under the best conditions, are fragile and in a constant state of flux. Early developers consciously kept this in mind when they preserved dunes and set homes well back from the ocean. But the new condominium developments were large structures built too close to the shore line, resulting in a steady erosion of a substantial portion of Hilton Head's beaches. And as the number of vacationers neared one million a year, water consumption went well above the national average. Growth brought more showers, baths, toilets, washing machines, and dishwashers. A great deal of fresh water also went to keeping golf courses and lawns green all year long. By the 1980s, salt water was beginning to intrude into the Floridan Aquifer under Parris Island.

More people and more business also meant more solid and liquid waste. It was not uncommon for some garbage and construction debris to be dumped in woods and marshes. Most household and business garbage was hauled off the island to landfills, but sewage had to be dealt with to prevent the contamination of the surrounding water, aquifer, and wildlife. Due to the economic building recovery after the 1974-1976 recession, the island's sewage treatment facilities were overloaded, and the state put a moratorium on new construction and closed shellfish beds in 1983. (The ban lasted only one year, and with the increased treatment capacity, building resumed.)

Unable to secure any assistance from the county, islanders realized the only remedy to their concerns would be to incorporate into a self-governing municipality. On May 10, 1983, citizens went to the poles and voted for the creation of the Town of Hilton Head Island.

The new town of Hilton Head Island is a saga way too multifaceted and complicated for this short history. To this day, if you ask islanders about the 1980s and early 1990s, they will roll their eyes and shake their heads. The founders were an elected body of political neophytes consciously trying to create a town in the wake of the island falling "victim to inept [plantation] management, changing absentee corporate policies, and a devastating combination of leveraged buyout, savings and loan hanky-panky and bankruptcy. What began with local community-minded builders [Fraser, Hack and McIntosh] ended in the hands of glib speculators and shady bankers who cared little about the plantations or Hilton Head" (M. N. Danielson, 1995). (By this time, Fraser had lost control of his Sea Pines and Hilton Head Plantation.) Then, soon after incorporation, the city's founders learned the building permits issued by the county could not be revoked or amended, thus allowing ugly, substandard complexes to be built. Next, a lawsuit was filed by the NAACP seeking an injunction on municipal actions because the Gullah of the island feared new zoning laws would mean not only higher taxes which they could not afford to pay, but density standards that would force the breakup of their family compounds. And when it seemed like the council was taking forever to pass a Land Management Ordinance, a "burn the bridge" group formed who wanted to stop all growth and development, and prevent the construction of the Cross Island Parkway. These, and a whole host of other issues, occupied city officials during the town's first twenty years.

More remarkably, the town has held fast to the principles Charles Fraser envisioned in wanting to "create something beautiful" by requiring that new development "exhibit a harmonious relationship with the natural environment by blending the principles of sensitive site planning, skillful architectural design, and an emphasis on landscaping that preserves and enhances the native vegetation. This "'Island Character'" is as much a process as it is an end product. It is also a philosophy about design; a philosophy that puts an emphasis on thorough consideration of all elements of a project."

To achieve this, here are a few guidelines that must be followed: A) Commercial structures must be set back away from main highways with vegetation buffers between the highway and buildings; B) Signs should serve to identify the business or development and not act as advertisements; also adequate landscaping must be provided to blend the sign into its surroundings; and C) When lighting is used, it should add to the visual quality of the development without detracting from the beauty of the night sky, and not interfere with sea turtle nesting. Furthermore, the Town has an aggressive land acquisition program to acquire land while it is still available to be held in perpetuity as wildlife preserves or believed to be needed by the public in the future for active and passive recreational uses and scenic easements. It also acquires already developed land or development rights in order to convert its use to a public use or to restore the property to open space. As of 2010, on the Island, the Town has purchased over 133 parcels, totaling over 1,177 acres of land.

Besides aesthetic concerns, town leaders recognize the native-Gullah islanders share a rich sense of history and family roots. They also realize any town plan must respect their past, but also must look forward and envision a future that reflects the shared aspirations and values of the people. For this reason, the planning process (in Ward One, where most Gullah live) began with broad input from residents to begin to establish a vision; a sense of direction which inspires and motivates the planning process. Based on the input of many residents who actively participated in the planning process, three basic principles have emerged as elements of a vision: Equity, Reconciliation, and Quality of Life. Main points include:

A) Encouraging Ward One residents to enter the economic mainstream of Hilton Head Island; B) Achieving greater representation in civic affairs; C) Retaining and transmitting native islander values and heritage; D) Retaining and enhancing neighborhood identity and historic features; E) Correcting deficiencies in basic services [in the neighborhoods of Gum Tree and Wild Horse Roads and Highway 278, only a small portion of this area contains sewer service]; and F) Moving toward a shared sense of community and identity as the Town of Hilton Head Island.

In Closing

Hilton Head is an island of historical significance, natural beauty, and character. It has endured its share of growing pains, and for the Gullah, displacement, but it has matured into a thriving community that plays host to over two million visitors each year. And as Virginia C. Holmgren wrote in her 1959 *Hilton Head: a Sea Island Chronicle*, "The past touches hands with the future on Hilton Head."

CODA

The Mystery of the GREYTON H. TAYLOR Monument

Photo courtesy Carla Sikorski Kirby @ 2018

A few years after I bought a home on Hilton Head, I began studying the island's history. I also made a point of locating and visiting all the historical markers scattered around the island. I was sure I had seen all of them until one day I was driving north on Wild Horse Road. About 350 yards away from Gumtree Road on the right, there is a stone and bronze monument about four feet high. (While not marked, today there are bright yellow-green crosswalk signs at the location.) I immediately turned around to investigate and discovered the following inscription:

GREYTON H. TAYLOR MEMORIAL FAMILY PARK. Dedicated to the people of Hilton Head Island this 24th day of April, 1992 by Muriel Fainder Taylor, in memory of her beloved husband, Greyton Hoyt Taylor, grape grower, wine maker, and farmer. A lover of the land.

My initial guess was that Greyton Taylor was in some way part of the Taylor Wine family of New York. But what was the story behind this monument that appears nowhere in any island guidebook? My first efforts in learning about the monument proved frustrating. Not only did no one on the island know who Greyton H. Taylor was, no one even knew of the monument's existence.

As it turned out, my first assumptions about Greyton Taylor proved correct. Greyton was the son of the founder of Taylor Wine Co. in Hammondsport N.Y. and managing partner from 1933-55. In 1958, Greyton began converting vineyards from native American grapes to French-American hybrid grape varieties which could withstand the region's cold winters. This act turned the State of New York into a leading wine producing region in the country.

In 1970, Greyton joined his son, Walter, to establish Bully Hill Winery on the site of the original Taylor Winery along the Keuka Lake (one of the New York Finger Lakes). For 20 years, he served as president of the Wine Conference of America, which represented wine companies throughout the country. Greyton also served as president of the Finger Lakes Wine Grower Association. He died on June 13, 1971 after a long illness.

Mr. Paul Sprague, museum director of the The Greyton H. Taylor Wine Museum in Hammondsport, N.Y., notes that Greyton built his winter home on Hilton Head Island in 1968. Being an avid fisherman and boater, Greyton enjoyed his winters in the South, returning to his home on Lake Keuka for the summers. With his passing in 1971, wife Mrs. Muriel Taylor spent most of her years in Sea Pines, although she did return occasionally to Hammondsport.

After Greyton's death, his wife, Muriel donated property they acquired on the north end of the island to the Town in 1991 with the provision that it only be used as a park. The monument was placed on the property and dedicated on April 24,1992.

In part, the Town Council resolution reads: *The Town of Hilton Head Island has received a gift of approximately five acres of real property located on Wild Horse Road on Hilton Head Island ... this gift was bestowed upon the Town by the Estate of Greyton H. Taylor and Mrs. Muriel F. Taylor with the condition that the land be used as a park and that this park be named the "Taylor Family Park" ... [the] Town Council gratefully accepts this donation of real property which will be named the Taylor Family Park and used solely as a park for residents and visitors alike for generations to come.*

The April 16, 1992 press release, announcing the dedication ceremony, states "The site will eventually be developed into a family-oriented park in recognition of Mr. Taylor's love for the land." It is sad to report this has not occurred. As so often happens when one mystery is solved, another one arises; in this case, "What happened to the park?"

The Wild Horse Road property was actually the home of a Native Island couple. The wife was the Taylor family's housekeeper for many years, with her husband employed part-time. Rumor and supposition suggests the couple had some financial issues, and while too proud to accept money, agreed to sell their property to the Taylors with the stipulation they could continue to live on the property, at no cost, until both passed away.

Not long after the couples' deaths, surviving relatives claimed the Town and/or the Taylors had stolen their family property. The dispute carried on long enough to cause the Town to defer any conversations about what to do with the property.

At one point, when the Town did pursue the idea of neighborhood parks, and one was proposed for this location, the Native Island community rejected this notion. They instead felt a park built on the banks of Skull Creek would be more beneficial. Due to hostile opposition, coupled with the lack of public use of the then recently built Green Shell Park off Squire Pope, the Town Council again tabled the idea of developing the Taylor Family Park.

Then about seven years ago, the construction of a not-for-profit community daycare center was proposed for the land. When the Town Council approached the Taylor Family with the idea, they objected to the plan as being inconsistent with the terms and intentions of the donation and dedication.

Consequently, "no other plans or ideas have been put forward for this property. Other capital project needs have continued to have higher priority" (Mr. Steve Riley, Hilton Head Island Town Manager).

So I guess the more meaningful question is, "What would be necessary to get the park built?" It would be admirable if the city would provide the money, but I am sure the cost would be prohibitive. Perhaps, the building of the GREYTON H. TAYLOR MEMORIAL FAMILY PARK could be a joint public-private venture? However the park is built, out of respect for the Taylor family, a way should be found.

Related YouTube video:
"Dedication of GHTaylor Memorial Park, Hilton Head Island, SC"

HILTON HEAD ISLAND TIME LINE

Used with permission from the Coastal Discovery Museum of Hilton Head Island.

Native American Occupation 8000 B.C. - 1500 A.D.

- 8000 B.C. - 1000 B.C. - Archaic Period Native Americans visited this area seasonally.
- 1335 A.D. Green's Shell Enclosure, a 4-foot-tall shell ridge that encloses 2 acres, was built along the banks of Skull Creek.

European Explorers 1500 - 1700

- 1521 - A Spanish expedition, led by Francisco Cordillo, explored this area, initiating European contact with local tribes.
- 1663 - Capt. William Hilton sailed from Barbados, on the Adventure, to explore lands granted by King Charles II to the eight Lords Proprietors. Hilton Head Island takes its name from a headland near the entrance to Port Royal Sound.
- 1698 - John Bayley, of Ireland, was given most of Hilton Head Island as a barony. Twenty-four years later, his son appointed Alexander Trench as his agent in charge of selling the land. For a short time, Hilton Head was called Trench's Island on some 18th century maps.

Plantation Era 1700 - 1860

- 1711 - Beaufort, South Carolina was founded.
- 1760s - Beaufort County's shipbuilding industry was one of the largest in the 13 colonies. The deep-water creeks around Hilton Head and the prevalence of hardwoods (like live oak) made the island a popular place for shipbuilding. The USS Constitution, "Old Ironsides," was rebuilt in 1997 using live oaks felled during construction of Hilton Head Island's Cross Island Parkway.
- 1779 - Privateers sailing with the British navy burned many houses on Skull Creek and around the island on their way to Beaufort and Charleston. Hilton Head residents tended to be Patriots, while Daufuskie residents were Tories.

- 1780 - Daufuskie Islanders burned several Hilton Head homes, including the Talbird home.
- 1788 - The Zion Chapel of Ease, a small wooden Episcopal church for plantation owners was constructed. All that remains is the cemetery, home to the Baynard Mausoleum, near Mathews Drive.
- 1790 - William Elliott II, of Myrtle Bank Plantation, grew the first successful crop of long-staple, or Sea Island, cotton in South Carolina on Hilton Head Island.
- 1813 - During the War of 1812, British forces landed on Hilton Head Island, burning many of the houses along Skull Creek.
- 1860 - There were more than 20 working plantations on the island before the Civil War. Most plantation owners did not live on Hilton Head. The island was populated with slaves and overseers.

The Civil War and the Union Occupation 1860 - 1865

- 1861 - Beginning in July, Fort Walker was built on Hilton Head Island at the entrance to Port Royal Sound in Order to protect the port from Union attacks.
- 1861 - On November 7th, Union forces attacked Fort Walker (later renamed Fort Welles in honor of Gideon Welles, secretary of the Navy) and Fort Beauregard in the Battle of Port Royal. Nearly 13,000 Union troops flooded onto the island in the days after the battle.
- 1862 - Hilton Head Island was also referred to as Port Royal, in reference to the Port Royal military installation. Port Royal was the home to the Department of the South.
- 1862 - Hilton Head's population swelled to over 40,000, including Union troops, civilian store-keepers, missionaries, prisoners of war, and slaves seeking refuge from their owners.
- One of the oldest structures on the island, the Queen Chapel, A.M.E. Church is located on Beach City Road. African Methodist-Episcopal missionaries founded the Queen Chapel in 1865. The original building has been a praise house used by slaves on the Pope plantation. The structure was updated in 1892 and 1952.1862 - Gen. Ormsby Mitchel

set up the town of Mitchelville to house the island's first freedman's village. Mitchelville residents elected their own officials, passed their own laws, and established the first compulsory education law in the state. The Mitchelville community was built along modern-day Beach City Road.

- 1862 - Fort Mitchel was built as a battery to protect Skull Creek from Confederate attacks. Fort Sherman, which circled the military installation, was completed.
- 1865 - The First African Baptist Church was founded in August. Several island churches formed out of this church, including St. James, Goodwill, Central Oakgrove, and Mt. Calvary.

Reconstruction and Isolation 1870s - 1940s

- 1868 - Large-scale military occupation of the island had ended. The island's population dropped to only a few thousand.
- 1870s -Some of Hilton Head Island's plantations were reclaimed by their antebellum owners after paying back taxes charged to their property. Other properties were held by the United States government, sold to speculators, or sold to freedmen who remained on the island after the Civil War.
- 1872 - The island was once again referred to as Hilton Head Island.
- 1893 - An enormous hurricane hit Beaufort County, killing at least 2,000 people in the county and flooding parts of the island with its 12-foot surge. Many of Hilton Head Island's structures were destroyed in this storm.
- 1901 - A 15-inch steam cannon was installed and tested on the beach at Coggins Point (modern-day Port Royal Plantation). It was 1 of 13 designed to protect the United States coast.
- 1917 - Troops were stationed at the former Union Fort Walker during World War I as lookouts for possible submarine attacks.
- 1920s - Gullah native islanders sailed bateaux from Hilton Head to the mainland, carrying people, crops, and livestock to the market on River Street in Savannah. Charlie Simmons

- Sr. operated the first mechanized ferry in 1930 from Simmons Fish Camp, located near Marshland Road.

- The Hilton Head Lighthouse was originally built by the Coast Guard in the 1870's. This lighthouse was built nearly 1 mile inland, and a smaller range lighthouse was built closer to the beach. Now, it is called the Leamington Lighthouse and is no longer used for navigation.1920s -The Hudsons and Toomers operated oyster factories on Hilton Head Island from the 1890s until the 1950s. By this time, the boll weevil had destroyed almost all of the Sea Island Cotton in the region.

- 1940 -The island's population was approximately 1,100 most of whom were descendants from freedmen who had made their homes on Hilton Head.

- 1941 -Marines were stationed at Camp McDougal near the Leamington Lighthouse. The lighthouse had been built in the 1870's and was known as the Hilton Head Lighthouse until the Palmetto Dunes development, Leamington, began. Marines paved the first road on the island, which ran from the ferry landing at Jenkins Island (now Outdoor Resorts) to the lighthouse.

Mainland Connection and Modern Era 1949-1990s

- 1949 - A group of lumber associates from Hinesville, Georgia, bought a total of 20,000 acres of pine forest on Hilton Head's southern end for an average of nearly $60 an acre. They formed The Hilton Head Company to handle the timber operation. The associates were Gen. Joseph B. Fraser, Fred C. Hack, Olin T. McIntosh, and C.C. Stebbins.

- 1950 - Logging took place on 19,000 acres of the island. There were three lumbermills built to harvest the timber. The island population was only 300 residents.

- 1950 - The first electricity was brought to the island by Palmetto Electric Cooperative.

- 1953 - A state-operated car ferry began running from Buckingham Landing (near Bluffton, on the mainland) to Jenkins Island (at Outdoor Resorts).

- 1954 - Hilton Head Elementary School opened for the island's black students. Isaac Wilborn was the principal of the elementary school from 1954 until it closed in 1974. The school was replaced by a new integrated school constructed on a new site in 1975.

- 1955 - Beaufort County state representative Wilton Graves opened the Sea Crest Motel on Forest Beach. At first, it consisted of two rooms. The first vacation cottages were developed on Folly Field Road.
- The J. Byrnes Bridge opened on May 20, 1956. This was the first bridge connecting Hilton Head to the mainland. The cost was $1.5 million. At first, the bridge cost $2.50 per round trip. The toll was phased out by 1959. The Byrnes Bridge was a swing bridge. It swung open to allow boats to pass through on either side of the center support.1956 - James F. Byrnes Bridge, a two-lane toll swing bridge, was constructed at a cost of $1.5 million. This opened the island to automobile traffic from the mainland. This year, forty-eight thousand cars traveled across the bridge. The toll was discontinued in December 1959.
- 1956 - Charles E. Fraser, bought his father's interest in The Hilton Head Company and began developing it into Sea Pines Plantation.
- 1956 - Norris and Lois Richardson opened the first supermarket on the island, located near Coligny Circle in the North Forest Beach area.
- 1956 - The Hilton Head Island Chamber of Commerce was established.
- 1958 - First deed to a lot in Sea Pines Plantation was signed. Beachfront lots initially sold for $5,350. By 1962, they were selling for $9,600.
- 1958 - Telephone service was offered by Hargray Telephone Company. The first Hilton Head office did not open until 1960.
- 1958 - Palmetto Bay Marina opened.
- 1960 - The island's first golf course, the Ocean Course, designed by George Cobb, was built in Sea Pines Plantation.
- 1961 - The McIntosh family subdivided 360 acres of The Hilton Head Company to start Spanish Wells.

- 1962 - Port Royal Plantation was developed by Hilton Head Company, led by Fred Hack.
- 1965 - The Sea Pines Medical Center was built. It was staffed by a retired doctor who lived in Sea Pines but served the entire island community.
- 1965 - Hilton Head Island had its first rural mail route established.
- 1967 - Sea Pines Plantation installed the island's first gates.
- 1967 - The Palmetto Dunes area was acquired from the Hilton Head Agricultural Company by Palmetto Dunes Corporation, headed by William T. Gregory, for $1,000 per acre.
- 1967 - The Hilton Head Airport opened.
- 1969 - Harbour Town village was completed. The full-time population of the island was 2,500.
- 1969 - The first Heritage Golf Classic played at Sea Pine's Harbour Town Links.
- 1970 - Island Packet newspaper was first published.
- 1970 - The Hilton Head Company started Shipyard Plantation.
- 1971 - Sea Pines acquired land on the north end of the island, which was developed into Hilton Head Plantation.
- 1974 - The swing-bridge was struck by a barge which force island residents to travel off the island on a pontoon bridge constructed by the Army Corps of Engineers. The bridge was closed for six weeks.
- 1975 - The island's full-time population by this time was 6,500. Over 250,000 visitors came to Hilton Head.
- 1975 - Hilton Head Hospital was completed.
- 1979 - Hurricane David missed the island, but high winds left beached eroded and destroyed several Singleton Beach homes.
- 1982 - A four-lane bridge was built to replace the two-lane swing-bridge to the island. The island's full-time population

was 12,500. More than 500,000 visitors came to Hilton Head in 1982.

- 1982 - Wexford Plantation and Long Cove Club were developed.
- 1983 - The Town of Hilton Head Island incorporated as a municipality.
- 1985 - Hilton Head's Comprehensive Plan was adopted by the town council. The population was over 17,000 full-time residents.
- 1985 - The Coastal Discovery Museum was established in 1985 with a mission to teach the public about the natural history and cultural heritage of the Lowcountry.
- 1987 - The town council passed the Land Management Ordinance of the Town of Hilton Head Island.
- 1989 - The Cross-Island Parkway project was approved. The Parkway's bridge spans Broad Creek and links the south end of the island to the north end.
- 1995 -The permanent year-round population exceeded 28,000 people. The island had over 1.5 million visitors.
- 1995 - Construction on the Cross-Island Parkway began.
- 1996 - The Master Land Use Plan for Ward One was started by the Town.
- 1997 - Cross Island Parkway opened in January. The total cost was $81 million for construction, land acquisition and planning.
- 1998 - Purchased 17 acres for the Fish Haul Creek Park (2005).
- 1998 - Dual Route Phase I and Dual Route Phase II road projects (1999).
- 1999 - Tax Increment Financing Districts are created.
- 1999 - South Beach Fill Renourishment Project.
- 1999 - Purchased 26 acres for the Shelter Cove Community Park (2001).

A New Century

- 2000 - Census population is 33,862.
- 2000 - Jarvis Creek Pump Station and South Forest Beach Phase I and Phase 2 (2001) Drainage Projects.
- 2000 - Opened new Fire Station #3 at 534 William Hilton Parkway.
- 2001 - Purchased 3 acres for the Green Shell Park (2004).
- 2001 - Purchased 3 acres for Compass Rose Park (2008).
- 2001 - Purchased 18 acres for the Mitchelville Beach Park (2007).
- 2001 - Purchased 13 acres for the Barker Field Expansion Recreational area (2006).
- 2001 - The International Building Codes (IBC) and amendments are adopted, and the Town converts from Southern Building Code to IBC.
- 2002 - The Coastal Discovery Museum relocated to Honey Horn after multi-million dollar public-private renovation/restoration effort.
- 2002 - The Town's Fire & Rescue received its 1st International Accreditation from the Commission on Fire Service Accreditation International and was the second in the state and the 53rd agency worldwide to be accredited.
- 2002 - Charles E. Fraser, the American real estate developer whose vision helped transform South Carolina's Hilton Head Island from a sparsely populated sea island into a world-class resort dies.
- 2003 - Opened new Fire Station #7 at 1001 Marshland Road.
- 2004 - Powerline burial project began.
- 2004 - Even-year elections for the Mayor and Town Council are adopted.
- 2004 - North Forest Beach Wexford Pump Station and North Forest Beach Phase II Drainage Project completed.
- 2005 - The U.S. Census Bureau Population estimate is 34,855.

- 2005 - Opened new Fire Station #4 at 400 Squire Pope Road.
- 2006 - The Disaster Recovery Commission is created and completed its work in 2012.
- 2006 - Atlantic Shorefront Fill Project.
- 2007 - The Town's Fire & Rescue received its 2nd International Accreditation from the Commission on Fire.
- 2007 - Office Park Road Realignment.
- 2007 - Pope Avenue pathway and boardwalks built.
- 2008 - Mathews Drive Corridor Improvements (roadway, pathway, drainage).
- 2009 - Coligny Beach Park Renovation is completed.
- 2009 - Opened the new Fire & Rescue Training Center at Dillon Road.
- 2009 - Opened the new Facilities Management Building at Gateway Circle.
- 2010 - Census population is 37,099.
- 2010 - The Town supported the Heritage Golf Tournament in year 2011 with a $1 million commitment.
- 2011 - Stormwater Utility is created countywide with significant Town leadership in the creation.
- 2011 - The Town committed funds for advertising to secure the RBC Heritage from 2012 to 2016.
- 2011 - Opened new Fire Station #5 at 20 Whooping Crane Way.
- 2011 - Port Royal Sound Shoreline Rehabilitation completed.
- 2012 - Town/Shelter Cove Town Center, LLC Developer Agreement for the redevelopment of the Mall at Shelter Cove is approved.
- 2012 - Town purchased a 23,500 square foot building on Shelter Cove Lane for the Beaufort County Sheriff's Office Island location.

- 2012 - The Town's Fire & Rescue received its 3rd International Accreditation from the Commission on Fire Service Accreditation International.
- 2012 - The Town's Fire & Rescue received the Heart Safe Community Award from the International Fire Chief's Association.
- 2013 - The Economic Development Corporation is created.
- 2013 - The former SHARE Center, now renamed the Hilton Head Island Senior Center, opens.
- 2013 - Opened new Fire Station #1 at 70 Cordillo Parkway.
- 2013 - Construction on new Fire Station #6 at the entrance to Palmetto Dune began.
- 2013 -Town celebrates its 30th Anniversary of Incorporation.
- 2015 - The Coastal Discovery Museum was recognized as a Smithsonian Affiliate.
- 2016 - Hilton Head Island inundated by massive Hurricane Matthew.
- 2017 - Hurricane Irma hilts Hilton Head Island.
- 2018 – The 50th annual RBC Heritage PGA TOUR golf tournament.

NOTES

i From Pope Ave., take either Cordillo Pkwy. or South Forest Beach Dr. to the Sea Pines Ocean gate. From the gate, drive south two streets, turning right onto Lawton Dr. At the third right, make a quick right, then left turn--the canal will be on the left. Drive straight back to the Sea Pines Forest Preserve on the right. Take the dirt road for .4 of a mile to Fish Island Picnic Area (also look for the Warner W. Plahs Wild Flower Field sign). The ring is just a short walk from the parking area.

ii To reach the Stoney-Baynard Ruins, refered to only as the "Baynard Ruins," from Pope Ave., turn onto Greenwood Dr. to the Sea Pines gate. Stay on Greenwood Dr. until Plantation Dr. and turn right. Take this until you come to a T in the road. Here, make a quick left, then a quick right--staying on Plantation Dr. almost its entire length. Ignore the sign that says "Baynard Park." Just stay on Plantation Dr. and "Baynard Ruins" is on the right. You will not see any ruins, rather you will only see a sign, a small dirt parking area and a bike rack. After parking, walk up the path and the main ruins will be on you left. This site can be a bit tricky to find, but it is well worth the effort!

iii Visitors are limited to the "Forts of Port Royal" tour conducted by the Coastal Discovery Museum at Honey Horn. Tours Reservations are required and can be made at the museum or by calling 843-689-6767.

iv To learn more about Gullah Heritage of Hilton Head Island, a visitor may wish to take a pleasant, narrated tour through several neighborhoods established during the Civil War, long "before the bridge" to the mainland. Call <u>Gullah Heritage Trail Tours</u> (843) 681-7066 or look for their orange flyers. Also, reservations can be made at the Coastal Discovery Museum.

The growth of historical and cultural tourism in the Lowcountry has brought increased interest in Gullah history and culture. Louise Miller Cohen, Founder and Director, and the other Board members of The Gullah Museum of Hilton Head Island, are currently raising funds for the restoration and preservation of several structures to depict Gullah life "before the bridge" to Hilton Head Island. When the museum is complete, visitors will be able to learn about Gullah history, culture, customs, traditions, language, stories, and songs. The first restored structure, "The Little House," also known as "Duey's Home" can be seen at the museum's future site at 12 Georgianna Drive at the intersection of Gumtree Road.

v Allison, AC. "Protection Afforded by Sickle-cell Trait Against Subtertian Malarial Infection". (FEB. 6, 1954). British Medical Journal.

vi I tried to track Mr. Stroud down for permission to us his photo but had no luck.

Sources

I would like to thank the Hilton Head Island-Bluffton Chamber of Commerce and the National Park Service for making available and granting permission to use much of the information found in The Gullah Heritage.

Archaic Period. Southeast Archeological Center, National Park Service Tallahassee, Florida.

Battle of Port Royal Fact Sheet. Coastal Discovery Museum, Hilton Head Island, SC.

Eliza Lucas Pinckney (1722–1793). South Carolina Business Hall of Fame.

Green's Shell Enclosure, Beaufort County. South Carolina Department of Archives and History.

Gullah Culture is Nothing Short of Uplifting. Hilton Head Island-Bluffton Chamber of Commerce.

Hilton Head Island: A Television History, 1996. DVD. South Carolina ETV.

Hilton Head Island Design Guide, 2003. Town of Hilton Head Island.

The History of Sea Island Cotton. Beaufort.com. Island Communications, Hilton Head Island, SC.

The Indian Shell Ring. Sea Pines Community Services Associates. Hilton Head Island, SC.

Mike Taylor's History of Hilton Head Island. CD. 1994. Brodie Media, Ltd., Bluffton, SC.

Mitchelville: Experiment in Freedom, 1995. Chicora Foundation, Inc., Chicora Foundation, Inc. Columbia.

Names in South Carolina 36 , 1972. Institute for Southern Studies, College of Arts and Sciences, University of South Carolina.

Pinckney Island NWR: Refuge History. 2009. U.S. Fish and Wildlife Service.

Profile: Charles Fraser. 1974. DVD. South Carolina ETV.

Sea Pines, Beaufort County. South Carolina Department of Archives and History.

Skull Creek, Beaufort County. South Carolina Department of Archives and History.

Town of Hilton Head Island Comprehensive Plan. May 4, 2010. Town of Hilton Head Island.

Woodland Period. Southeast Archeological Center, National Park Service Tallahassee, Florida.

Campbell, Emory, *Gullah Cultural Legacies*. 2008. BookSurge Publishing.

Carse, Robert, *Department of the South: Hilton Head Island in the Civil War*. 1976. State Printing Company.

Carota, Buzz, *The Evolution of a Town, Hilton Head Island, South Carolina*. 2002. Data Reproductions Corporation.

Cross, Wilbur, *Gullah Culture in America*. 2012. John F. Blair, Publisher, Winston-Salem, North Carolina.

Danielson, Michael N., *Profits and Politics in Paradise: The Development of Hilton Head Island.* 1995. University of South Carolina Press, Columbia, South Carolina.

Dor-Ner, Zvi , William Scheller, *Columbus and the Age of Discovery.* 1991. William Morrow & Co.

Fraser, Charles, E., *The Art of Community Building.* No publication date or publisher.

Greer, Margaret, *The sands of time: A history of Hilton Head Island.* 2004. SouthArt, Inc., Hilton Head Island, South Carolina.

Hefter, Natalie, editor, *Images of America, Hilton Head Island.* 1998. Arcadia Publishing, Charleston, South Carolina.

Heide, Gregory and Russo, Michael, "Investigation of the Coosaw Island Shell Ring Complex (38BU1866)." 2003. South Carolina Department of Natural Resources Heritage Trust Program.

Hemmings, E. Thomas, "Emergence of Formative Life on the Atlantic Coast of the Southeast." 1970. Institute of Archaeology and Anthropology, South Carolina.

Holmgren, Virginia C., *Hilton Head, A sea Island Chronicle.* 1959. Hilton Head Island Publishing Company, Hilton Head Island, South Carolina.

Hypes, Jannette, "Gullah: A Language, a Life, a Living History." 2006. YAHOO! VOICES.

Insley, Bob, "The Steamgun." Coastal Discovery Museum, Hilton Head Island, SC.

Lawrence, David R. and Wrightson, Hilda L., "Late Archaic-Early Woodland Period Shell Rings of the Southeastern United

States Coast: A Bibliographic Introduction." 1989. Institute of Archaeology and Anthropology, South Carolina.

Lowe, William C., "Battle of Port Royal." 2001. America's Civil War (historynet.com).

Michie, James L., "An Archeological Investigation of the Cultural Resources of Callawassie Island, Beaufort County, South Carolina."1982. Institute of Archaeology and Anthropology, South Carolina.

Muller, Barbara, "Eliza Lucas Pinckney and the Indigo Bonanza." 2010. Glimpses, The Heritage Library, Hilton Head Island SC.

Musicant, Ivan, *Divided Waters: The Naval History of the Civil War*. 1995. Harpercollins, New York, NY.

National Park Service. *Low Country Gullah Culture Special Resource Study and Final Environmental Impact Statement*. 2005. Atlanta, GA: NPS Southeast Regional Office.

Opala, Joseph, "The Gullah: Rice, Slavery and the Sierra Leone Connection" website, Gilder Lehrman Center, Yale University.

Rankin, Richard, *A New South Hunt Club*. 2012. Willow Hill Press.

Rowland, Lawrence S., Rogers, George C., Moore, Alexander, *The History of Beaufort County, South Carolina: 1514-1861*. 1996. University of South Carolina Press.

Rutt, *Richard H., William E. Cornelia, and Gary K. Chapman, Hilton* Head Island: A perspective. 1975. Cornelia, Rutt, Chapman.

Russo, Michael, "Archaic Shell Rings of the Southeast U.S. National Historic Landmarks Historic Context." 2002.

Southeast Archeological Center, National Park Service Tallahassee, Florida.

Russo, M. and Heide, G., "Shell rings of the southest US" (2001). Antiquity 75, Tallahassee, Florida.

Shuler, Kristrina A. and Ralph Bailey, Jr., "A History of the Phosphate Mining Industry in the South Carolina Lowcountry." Brockington and Associates, Inc. Mount Pleasant, South Carolina.

Sumpter, Althea, "Geechee and Gullah Culture." (2004-2012). Georgia Humanities Council and the University of Georgia Press web site.

Tetzlaff, Monica M., "Mitchelville: An Early Experiment in Self Governance," In The Forgotten History: Hilton Head During the Civil War." 1993. Charles C. McCracken and Faith M. McCracken eds. Time Again Publication. Hilton Head Island, SC.

Trinkley, Michael, "Archaeological Survey of Hilton Head Island, Beaufort County, South Carolina." 1987. Chicora Foundation, Inc., Columbia, South Carolina.

Trinkley, Michael B. (ed.), "Indian and Freedman Occupation at the Fish Haul Site (38BU805), Beaufort County, South Carolina." 1986. Chicora Foundation, Inc. Research Series 7. Columbia, South Carolina.

West, Jean M., "The Devil's Blue Dye: Indigo and Slavery." Slaveryinamerica.org.

West, Jean M., "King Cotton: The Fiber of Slavery." Slaveryinamerica.org.

Wooster, Lyman, "Hilton Head's Economy in the 18th and 19th Centuries." 2010. Glimpses, The Heritage Library, Hilton Head Island SC.

Wright, Louis Booker, *South Carolina: A Bicentennial History*. 1976. W W Norton & Co Inc.

David B. McCoy earned his history teaching degree from Ashland University and his graduate degree from Kent State University. After teaching thirty-two years, David retired to write short books on a wide variety of topics. He also holds certificates of completion from FEMA and the Columbia Regional Learning Center for personal emergency preparedness.

Royalties are donated to nonprofits organizations.

Ebooks are available from Amazon and Barnes & Noble, and paperbacks ** only from Amazon.

- *100 Plus Ways to Protect Your Privacy***
- *The Average Family's Multi-Disaster Preparedness Manual***
- *A Short History of Hilton Head Island***
- *Gullah Culture: 1670—1950.*** (The Gullah are the descendants of enslaved Africans who live in the Lowcountry region of the South. The Gullah people have been able to preserve much of their African cultural heritage because of geography, climate, and patterns of importation.)
- *Christopher Gist*** (Gist is remembered for exploring lands west of the Appalachian Mt. and opening up of the Ohio Country in the 1700s.)
- *George Washington* (HarperPress, $1.99. Audible Audio Edition, $2.95.)
- *The Kent State Shootings and What Came Before***

- *An American's Guide to Understanding the Troubles of Northern Ireland.***
- *England's First Industrial Revolution*
- *General John Burgoyne: general, statesman, playwright* **
- *The Poems of Francis Scott Key, Ed. By David B McCoy*
- *Moon Crater Shorty: A novella of Dada-like proportions***
- *Seeds of Change: three long poems***(Paper only)
- *The Sippo Lake Collection & Other Poems***(Paper only)
- *Andrew Jackson*
- *Francis Scott Key*
- *Oliver Hazard Perry: The Hero of Lake Erie*
- *Dolley Madison, Gilbert Stuart, and George Washington's Portrait*
- *The 1920s: The Rise of Modern America*
- *The 1920s: Early Jazz and the Harlem Renaissance*
- *The 1920s: Margaret Sanger and the Birth Control Movement*
- *The 1920s: The Invisible Empire of the Ku Klux Klan*
- *The 1920s: The Scopes Monkey Trial*

- *The 1920s: Volumes 1 - 5: The Rise of Modern America; Early Jazz and the Harlem Renaissance; Margaret Sanger; The Ku Klux Klan; The Scopes Monkey Trial*** (Paper only)

- *Charlemagne: volume one: Carolingian Dynasty Rise to Power and the Saxon war*
- *Charlemagne: volume two: The Daily Lives of Peasants*
- *Charlemagne: volume 3: Becoming Holy Roman Emperor*
- *Charlemagne: volume 4: Carolingian Renaissance*
- *Charlemagne: Volumes 1-4***(Paper only)

sparechangepress.com

Massillon, Ohio

scp-iyh-staff@yandex.com

Made in the USA
Middletown, DE
28 May 2019